EXPOSING THE
REJECTION MINDSET

EXPERIENCE LOVE

KNOW WHO YOU ARE

EMPOWER YOUR RELATIONSHIPS

MARK DEJESUS

Exposing the Rejection Mindset
Experience Love | Know Who You Are | Empower Your Relationships
By Mark DeJesus
Turning Hearts Ministries & Transformed You
www.markdejesus.com
© 2018 – Mark DeJesus & Turning Hearts Ministries
Published by: Turning Hearts Ministries
ISBN: 978-1981594610
Cover Design: Avanska Design and 99designs.com
Editorial Assistance Provided by: Stan Doll and Melissa DeJesus

CONTENTS

DEDICATION

This book is dedicated to every heart that is willing to face the issues of their heart and go deeper with God.

I especially dedicate this book to my family, that generations to come will be freed from the chains of rejection. May every tool meant to hold us back be destroyed and eradicated.

INTRODUCTION
A Call for Change in How We Do Relationships

God is in the business of healing and restoring our relationships like never before. The struggles we all face reveal the need for us to grow deeper in love and stronger in how we face relationship challenges.

God is a Father, so His highest priority is to mature us as His sons and daughters. We demonstrate that maturity the most when we walk in powerful and fruitful relationships. The more we grow in how we relate to one another, the greater we can stand as one when the storms rage against us.

But I am not going to sugar coat it. This is so much easier said than done.

Look at most of the struggles you face in life. Odds are most of them surround the world of your relationships. What makes you angry? What are you disappointed about? What losses and attacks are you recovering from? What do you lose sleep about the most? What issues create the most stress and discomfort?

The answers to those questions reveal the battles taking place over how we see ourselves and those around us. The health of our hearts and fruit we experience hinge on how well we handle these battles. The spiritual attacks we face reveal our greatest potential, but also our greatest vulnerabilities. If we don't make changes soon, we'll crumble under the rubble of relationship meltdowns.

THE NEED FOR RELATIONSHIP HEALING

Years ago, I set out to share my passion for heart healing and transformation to the masses. In my heart, I couldn't help but sense a Red Cross sign over the doorposts of churches and communities. I was sobered by the desperate need that churches had to experience heart healing and relationship restoration.

The problem is that the people of God were not necessarily seeing the importance of this need. Too many were content to live as spiritual zombies, going through the motions without vibrant life or fruitfulness. So many were not even aware that their unaddressed brokenness was sabotaging their effectiveness. Others just ignored the deep-rooted problems that were festering in their life. By the time they were made aware of any relationship problems, the destruction already had a massive negative impact.

My journey has taken me into a wide variety of settings, where challenges and difficulties of all kinds are present. From working out communication issues in a business setting, to mediating strife-filled situations amongst church members, I've rolled up my sleeves in some of the most heartbreaking dilemmas. I have also witnessed some the most abusive actions coming out of the most unexpected people.

Because of what I do in helping people, I have witnessed first-hand the broken down relational world that exists behind the scenes. Some of the most impressive organizations or families on the outside can have a world of hidden dysfunction festering behind the curtain. Sadly, the devastation seems to be getting more intense.

This has really sobered my heart to face my own personal brokenness with greater awareness and tenacity. It has also put a passion in my heart to sound the alarm. If we don't do something soon, many more hearts will erode in brokenness and more believers will be taken out. When we take the healing of our broken areas seriously, dramatic change and eternal impact can manifest. But we need to come to terms with how our relational wounds are affecting our lives.

PULLING BACK THE CURTAIN

I have made acquaintances with folks that did not appear to be broken from an outside glance. Their marriages and families resembled the "cookie cutter" picture we all dream of attaining. Yet beneath their exterior were trails of unresolved pain and bondage. These struggles festered under the surface and eventually exploded into public view. Yet most are shocked when the truth comes out and family issues are brought into the light.

More people than I care to admit are dissolving from the inside out. Some situations are more outwardly evident, while others are hidden behind various masks and false personas.

It is important to note that the majority of people I am talking about are professing Christians. These are well-intentioned believers who slowly eroded spiritually, emotionally and even physically, never realizing their God-given potential.

These tragic stories did not occur overnight. The breakdown took place slowly over the course of time. I was no longer surprised to hear that there were deep addictions, marital division or high levels of mental illness taking place in the lives of people that I crossed paths with every day.

There were people in the church that no one seemed to know how to help or even how to deal with. Included in this group were those who constantly lacked mental peace or others who just could not find healing to their struggles in life.

There were those who had been deeply wounded in their past or were abused during their upbringing and had no idea how to resolve their painful history. I found a large percentage of well-meaning saints dabbling in hidden addictions: illegal and legal drugs, pornography, gambling, eating disorders or other vices.

ASSESSING THE DAMAGE

I also witnessed the dysfunctional relational patterns exhibited by many. The impact of these behaviors on others in the community had a massive ripple effect. With no resources to help them, these people were just tolerated or avoided by those around them.

Amongst these challenging scenarios were people who constantly desired the spotlight and passionately looked for ways to get the attention of others. There were those who were so needy, they drained the emotions of everyone and left those they came in contact with exhausted with their never-ending need to be validated.

There were many who seemed to magnetically attract conflict everywhere they went. It seemed to follow their every move. They would leave a church and bring their baggage to a new one. It seemed the more you reached out to them in an attempt to move towards resolution, the worse the situations got. What was said in love was not even being heard. This miscommunication yielded anger and gossip was spread. In the process, the names of good-intentioned people, who were only trying to help bring healing to the situation, were maligned.

Pastors and church leaders are not immune from these problems. In fact, their unaddressed brokenness infected many in their tribe with multiplying impact. The brokenness of the heart can be hidden for only so long until it seeps out and pollutes how people in the church engage.

GETTING TO THE ROOT SYSTEM

As a researcher of root issues and their effects on people's lives, it is clearly evident to me that there is a common core problem that exists amongst our daily battles. The patterns I have described all involve relational breakdown to some degree. Many times, these breakdowns come out of a place where love has been lacking or compromised in someone's life. The majority of problems that lead someone to seek help from a counselor, therapist, pastor or leader typically involve some form of relational breakdown.

Many times, people lacked healthy love relationships and the damage from being "unloved" was breeding a toxic way of thinking. These individuals tend to see the world through a lens clouded by pain, like a smearing of mud that keeps their vision from being sound and clear. They tend to project stories onto others based on their past hurt, while blaming their predicaments on everyone else. The reality is that deep down inside, large voids exist that have never been fulfilled or satisfied.

The toxic root system that is a common denominator is *the rejection mindset.* For years, I have been exposing people to the dangers of this hidden, yet sadistic mindset. Rejection's mission is quite simple. It involves disconnecting you from the power of love, who you are in your identity and from experiencing life changing relationships. Exposing its tentacles may be one of the most freeing experiences of your life.

TWO CHOICES LEFT FOR US ALL

I am very certain that people will find themselves in one of two groups when it comes to transformation in the years ahead. Those in the first group will take the painful experiences in life, shove them down, deny them or spiritualize them away. They will continue to put on a false front to the world, dive into their busy lives and use avoidance at every opportunity. They will make sure they never have to deal with the broken areas of their heart.

On the contrary, the second group will be very courageous. They will recognize the pain in their life and be willing to walk through a process that allows for change and renewed living. As a part of their journey, they will take personal responsibility for change, preferring to be whole rather than living in denial. They will allow God to perform a powerful, yet sometimes uncomfortable process of authentic transformation from the inside out. They will submit themselves to reworking how they deal with and process relationships on all levels.

The decision is, what group will you be in? Will you make the decision to let God upgrade how you do relationships? Or will you look away, hoping the problems will just disappear?

For those who want the upgrade. Keep reading…

THE WAR OVER RELATIONAL HEALTH

E verything in your life rises and falls on your ability to live in healthy relationships. Your spiritual health, emotional wellness, mental stability and even physical health are all impacted by the quality of your relationship with:

- God
- Yourself
- The world around you.

All three relationships need to be wrapped in the power of love for you to manifest an abundant life. Yet so many assume that these areas should manifest love fairly easy, with little drama or few problems. This is why discouragement sets in so quickly, because many are unaware of the spiritual battles that wage over their relationships.

We scratch our heads when conversations go sour, motives are questioned, communication is twisted and hearts are hardened. We wonder why rational discussions don't resolve conflict and we fall prey to division so easily. What could become amazing connections can make a turn for the worse overnight. So, what is going on here?

I believe that most people genuinely love each other, but they cannot fully engage connection with others because an invisible war is interfering. If you have been ignorant of the spiritual battle, now would be a good time to sober up and realize your relationship world is under attack. It is time to recognize we have fallen asleep at the wheel and awaken our spiritual senses to the battle that is waging over our relationships.

The battle is pretty simple. Most people get lost in an emotional dodge ball match with others because they don't realize how the enemy has gotten into their relationship patterns. The adversary latches onto areas of personal brokenness in your life and hooks it into another person's brokenness, to keep you from ever having fruitful connection.

GOD'S DESIGN FOR RELATIONSHIPS

God created and designed us to function in healthy relationships on three levels. The first dimension is our love relationship with God (*"You shall love the Lord your God"* Mark 12:30).

A love relationship with God begins by learning to *receive* His love. (*"We love Him because He first loved us."* 1 John 4:19)

Most honest believers I speak with have a genuine struggle receiving love from God. This is critical, because out of receiving love from Him, we are able to love God back in response.

The second dimension is with yourself. This is where we have not been equipped the most. God's design is for us to love ourselves as His creation. A great way to see that you have received God's love is you are able to love yourself. *("Love your neighbor as yourself"* Mark 12:31) Loving yourself comes into agreement with how God sees you. You are His workmanship and wonderful masterpiece, called to be a dwelling place of the Holy Spirit.

Third, love has its greatest fulfillment when we take the love we have received from God and give it out freely to others *("Love your neighbor"* Mark 12:31).

But don't miss this. All three areas are under attack. In fact, my personal work with thousands of people show they struggle with receiving love from God, loving themselves and being able to love people without interference.

YOU WERE MADE FOR LOVE

God's highest priority is love. That's because He is love. He doesn't just have love, He is the very essence of love. When you experience love in life, it is for the purpose of leading you to Himself. If you want to see God's nature manifested on this planet, then we need to learn the power of love that is like nothing else.

Not only has God created us for love, He has given us many tools that are effective in healing the areas of our lives that lack love's presence. He does not leave us stranded.

There are many practical ways we can address our struggle with love, but it takes a hunger and teachable spirit to engage them.

THE SPIRITUAL SHIFT IN MY LIFE

Years ago, I plunged into a deep reformation in my Christian walk, which was first initiated by a personal breakdown that hit me square in the face. Anxiety, depression and deep struggles of the mind were overtaking me. It was during this time that I began to see that the love of God was missing in my daily experience. I also became aware of how much I was under siege with thoughts that kept me bound.

In a posture of surrender, I began to seek God's Word at a deeper level, in an effort to understand what was driving my personal battles. I needed some real answers and was feeling very discontented with the current Christian clichés. I wanted truth, even if it made me uncomfortable. As I read the Scriptures, I asked God to show me what I had been missing.

I specifically remember praying out loud, *"God, if there is something I am missing in Your Word that I need, please expose it to me. If there is truth that I need to engage that I am blind to, I ask that you reveal it to me, even if it makes me uncomfortable."* Little did I know, that would be one of the most effective prayers I have ever prayed. The Scriptures opened up to me like I was reading them for the first time.

It was as if a veil was taken off my eyes. The Bible became more than just a nice book with great stories and "good-boy" rules. My vision was awakened to the spiritual life that the

Scriptures point to. It was like I was given a pair of spiritual glasses as I was reading the Word. It wasn't just stories; I was receiving a lens on how to see!

One thing that became immediately apparent was the spiritual war going on all around me; a battle I had too often neglected when addressing hindrances and struggles. I looked around and very few people seemed to be engaging the spiritual battle. Most people were not even acknowledging it and many were living in a world of denial.

I came to realize these relational breakdowns all around were not just natural occurrences. They were spiritually orchestrated by the enemy and carried out with intentional strategy. The same problems followed through generations of families and spilled over into the lives of those they came in contact with. Becoming awakened to the spiritual war that surrounded me was the first step in getting leverage to heal and walk into greater freedom.

EXPOSING THE HINDERING MINDSET

During that personal awakening in my life, I was serving in a pastoral role at a large church. I knew I was in desperate need for transformation, as my lack of peace was at an all-time high. I also saw that most believers were in similar places. Unfortunately, they continued to jump on the same religious merry-go-rounds, from which they were seeing no fruit or change.

During a particular teaching series at our church, the emphasis was on the book of Romans. As I studied along in the series, I found myself having a personal revival in the eighth chapter.

It was at this point that I came face to face with the toxic mindset that was plaguing my life and the lives of those all around me. Romans 8:15 laid it out clearly for me. The bondage I had been carrying all my life was right here.

For you did not receive the spirit of bondage again to fear, but you received the Spirit of adoption by whom we cry out, "Abba, Father." Romans 8:15

I nearly jumped out my chair and exclaimed, *"This is what's been holding me back!"* The scales on my eyes fell as I began to see what had bound me for so long. I heard loudly in my heart, *"this is rejection."*

The basis for a spirit of bondage is **rejection,** which is the opposite of adoption. Some translations communicate this bondage as a *spirit that makes us a slave to fear.* It seeks to keep us in continual bondage by perpetuating **a rejection mindset.**

THE ENEMY OF ADOPTION

Adoption communicates acceptance, love and identity. It's God eternal message to empower His sons and daughters. Rejection brings a counterfeit message to block or distort God's love and our awareness of identity in His love.

In studying thousands of believers over the years, I have found that rejection has greatly interfered with their Christian foundation. They initially came to God on the basis of His love and acceptance, but then began to live out their spiritual life trying to perform and earn a sense of love, value and acceptance. I know this well because it was my experience.

When I saw what a rejection mindset was doing, not only was my heart illuminated, my lens on life shifted almost overnight. I have never been the same since. I began to immediately see where rejection had been my way of thinking for most of my life. The branches of this root system began to unfold before me and I quickly saw its impact on my life and previous generations.

It became obvious how this rejection was infecting relationships all around me. It had placed a cap over the potential of many. Marriages, homes, workplaces, communities and churches were exhausting their resources dealing with the weeds of relational breakdown. In attempts to remedy these situations, the church would try to address behaviors that were manifesting, by plucking a bad branch, only to find it quickly grew back again, because the root of rejection was never addressed and uprooted.

STEPPING OUT TO HELP PEOPLE

As Melissa and I shared our heart and passion for people to be healed and free, we noticed that communities of all kinds had been deeply infested with a rejection mindset. Leaders were drained and burned out because of unresolved rejection issues in the organization. At the same time, the leader's own rejection issues were leaking into the daily activities of the organization.

Counseling session after counseling session only produced more weariness and less transformation. Our hearts wept as we saw relationships with phenomenal potential crumble to the ground, usually because of a rejection issue. To top it off, I watched as unresolved rejection took out key leaders in ministry. Pastors and very influential people were taken out by struggles that went unattended for decades, eventually exploding at the worst possible point.

During this time, I began to develop a holy anger for what the enemy was doing in the body of Christ. A fire was burning inside of me to see this meticulous plot exposed so that people could take back their identity and love relationships for good!

Despite our intentions, those same people we worked with often lashed out against us. As we all know, hurting people will hurt people, even those that are tending to their wounds.

This passion further intensified as Melissa and I pastored a local church. Here again, we watched rejection push its agenda and thwart the fruitful stages of what God wanted to do. We watched that as soon as certain relationships would show the potential to go to the next level and become long-term, covenant relationships, rejection would rise up and erode them.

A CALL FOR AWAKENING

I write everything for the sole purpose of seeing other people free. I have made a commitment to God that whatever He teaches me, I will share with everyone He leads me to.

I know this: the devil hates seeing loving, healthy, vibrant and fruitful relationships in the church. We must recognize the war against it or we may find ourselves collapsing from the inside out.

Jesus warned us that the last days would be filled with intense relationship struggles. As part of this breakdown in society, He spoke clearly that many people will be more easily offended. They will also betray each other. Relationships will be filled with hate, where people will withdraw and love less.

This will give greater rise to false prophets who will deceive people. Many people's perceptions and lifestyles will be based on these deceptions, being nothing more than a counterfeit. Because of this lawlessness, their ability to walk in love will grow cold (Matthew 24:10-13). This is a serious issue that is already at work.

Rejection is one of the primary tools to destroy our love capacity. Satan knows that if we feel absent or separated from love, we will lose connection to the key for all personal sanity. Therefore, it is of high importance that we first deal with the struggles in our own life that keep us from bountiful relationships. It will help us gain an empowered spiritual lens and equip us to deliver authentic love to those in bondage.

TWO CRITICAL QUESTIONS

Everyone is born with key questions in their heart. When these questions are not answered in a healthy and solid manner, a rejection mindset forms within us. These two questions are: *Who am I?* and *Am I loved?*

All of the personal battles you face come down to your sense of relational safety and how secure you are in your identity. Most people spend their time covering over these two areas, yet they are the root system that determine the health of your life.

Love addresses our sense of safety. *Do you feel loved in relationships? Do you feel you matter?*

Identity addresses our sense of security. *Do you know who you really are? Are you firmly connected to what God says about you?*

GETTING TO THE ROOT

The fact that you are reading this means you desire to walk in greater wholeness. In order to experience this, we have to be willing to address the underlying belief systems that influence everything. When we face the root system with courage, we allow a dynamic healing experience to unfold. When the ax comes to the root, the rest of the toxic branch structure begins to wither away. As John the Baptist said, *"And even now the ax is laid to the root of the trees."* (Luke 3:9a)

THE DEEPEST TOXIC ROOT

The deepest root hindrance that inflicts the greatest amount of damage is the root of rejection. This toxic mindset trains people to live in ways that are consistent with rejection-based thinking.

Of course, everyone has to deal with being rejected in life. **What I am working diligently to uncover is a rejection mindset and its assault to separate us from love, identity and healthy relationships.**

START WITH YOURSELF

As a warning, before you go pointing out everyone's rejection issues, you need to see it in your own life. When

18

the light switch comes on, it's an exciting experience, but one that will sober you to the core. Millions of believers every day are living with a lesser identity and a diluted experience of love. This is a tragic plague that must be addressed.

Helping others does not involve pointing out their rejection issues, but in demonstrating your own personal recognition and healing journey. Please don't mistake it, my writing is not directed at everyone else. It's for you, because you are the only person you can change.

The greatest fruit I see in relationships is when I am able to stop looking at what others need to change and say, *"God, grow me up and change ME."* So, the question is, *"Are you willing to face the rejection mindsets you may have?"*

QUESTIONS FOR CONSIDERATION

1. How would you describe the health of your relationships? With God? With others? With yourself?
2. Where do you see the greatest battle when it comes to your relationships?
3. In learning about a rejection mindset, where have you seen its influence in your life?
4. When it comes to the question, *"who am I?"* How would you answer that?
5. What about *"Am I loved?"* What comes up in your heart when you ask that question?

PRAYER

Father God, I thank You that You made me for relationships and to be filled with love. I was created to be loved and to love. You designed with me an identity and purpose. I know it is Your desire for me to walk in fruitful relationships, so I give you room to work on my heart and help me heal where I need to be healed.

I ask that You help me to see where rejection has stolen and blocked my ability to experience love to its fullest. Allow me to see the lies, so I can expose them and drive them out with your love and truth.

I ask that through this process, You would give me eyes to see so that my heart can experience a deeper dimension of love. Heal me, grow me and set me free. May I experience love and a new level of identity security. In Jesus name, amen.

WHAT IS A REJECTION MINDSET?

Experiencing rejection from someone can be incredibly painful. Yet there is nothing deadlier to relational health than living with a rejection mindset. When a rejection mindset is in operation, it doesn't matter if someone actually rejects you or not, you still feel rejection. It is a virus that masses of people are infected with, often without realizing it. Meanwhile, it is behind just about every relationship breakdown and the collateral damage that ensues.

It's important for you to understand that rejection is not just something that happens to you. It is a mindset that will infiltrate your every thought, perception and motive. I have never met a person who will not have to face this monster and do business with rejection-based perspectives in their life. Its tentacles will slither in quietly, wrapping itself around your thinking while leaving you defeated by negative circumstances.

Take a look at every broken relationship, church split, divorce, midlife crisis and nervous breakdown and you will find a rejection mindset there. It will leave a trail of destroyed relationships and divided communities in its path.

Rejection will keep us in a vortex of our unaddressed brokenness, repeating the cycles until we allow ourselves to engage in personal healing. Unless we recognize the deception of rejection and remove its patterns from our life, we will always live under a limited story. What makes a rejection mindset dangerous is that it follows you until you kick it out.

Identity struggles abound in our society, showing the rampant work of rejection-based thinking. Generations of people wander through life disconnected from love and who God says they are.

Meanwhile, so many of us struggle with what it means to be loved and feel affirmed. Relationships become challenging when you have not been solidified in love and healthy connection. Rejection teaches you to earn love and acceptance or to not bother trying at all. Most people bounce back and forth between the two.

A PERSONAL WRESTLING MATCH

A major aspect of my personal transformation involved driving a rejection mindset out of my life. It took hunger and honest assessment to see the influence it was having on me. Over time, I realized the majority of my life was actually influenced by rejection.

Ask yourself a few questions and you can find rejection's deception:

- *Do I feel the peace of God's love?*
- *Can I easily experience His unconditional love?*
- *Do I love myself?*
- *Am I connected to healthy love in my relationships?*
- *How do I go about feeling loved today?*
- *How do I get my value on a daily basis?*
- *What is the thing that people do to me that bothers me the most?*
- *How do I deal with pain in life?*

Most people live their life according to a limited identity. Their confidence is low and many of their styles of relating can be very dysfunctional. The problem is we are so conditioned with just getting by, we don't see the greater potential, nor the hindering mindsets that are in the way.

REJECTION'S MISSION

Rejection's number one mission is to project a sense of separation from the love of the Father. If you have ever felt far from God, rejection is often behind those thoughts and impressions. If you feel distant from love, you will also lack a sense of identity, because the only way to know who you are is to be connected to the Father's loving heart.

When rejection operates in someone's life, it will project a false sense of reality. A swarm of lies envelop, making a person believe God does not love them, people do not love them and life is always working against them.

A DEADLY ROOT SYSTEM

A rejection mindset creates a system of thinking which seeps into many areas of relationships. When its lies are removed, a toxic lens gets taken off and a whole new vision can open up. We become free to let our true identities shine authentically, with less drama and little torment. We become free to love without any conditions or toxic attachments. In addition, the greatest gift of being free from rejection is that we can truly live as ourselves.

TWO MAIN TARGETS

There are two main foundational issues that rejection seeks to corrode. *The first is to prevent the unconditional love of Father God from being experienced.* Knowing *about* God's love does not bring the change. Experiencing it does. To possess a heart connection with the love of God is the greatest experience available. Those who struggle in any way to know, feel and experience the love of God, often have a rejection mindset.

The second key area that rejection attacks is our identity. Knowing who we are as sons and daughters is what we stand on in the midst of battle. You collapse in the battle when you are disconnected to who you are. A rejection mindset will train us to find identity outside of God's love and acceptance; driving us to seek success, societal affirmation or achievement for fulfillment.

REJECTION DETECTION QUIZ

As you have been reading, you may be wondering, if you have rejection working in your life. Here are some basic questions to help identify where rejection often contaminates people. If you answer them honestly, you can position yourself to recognize rejection's work and step into greater transformation. Take a moment to mark which symptoms could apply to you.

- *Do you struggle with feeling far from God? (Find yourself saying, "I feel far from God's presence" or "God seems far from me.")*
- *Is experiencing God's love a struggle?*
- *Do you only feel good if you are doing something productive or achieving something?*
- *Do you find yourself trying to please God with your behavior?*
- *Do you feel ignored by friends, family, leaders?*
- *Do you feel uncomfortable in social settings, where you either put on a mask or stumble through interactions all together?*
- *Do you anticipate rejection from new people you meet?*
- *Do you feel like if people knew the real you, they would not like you?*
- *Do you become easily hurt and offended by people?*
- *When someone questions you or disagrees with you, do you become deeply irritated, angry and argumentative? Do you feel a need to be right in discussions?*
- *Do you "over-talk" in social settings? Do you tend to not talk at all?*
- *Do you repeatedly feel compelled to tell others about the accomplishments you have achieved or flash your resume when you talk to people?*
- *Is your worth and value based on how well you do something?*
- *Do you do things to get attention from people?*
- *Do you struggle with addictive habits?*
- *Do you find yourself comparing yourself to others?*

- *Do you have a hard time figuring out where you are headed in life?*
- *Or, are you highly driven, performance oriented and achievement motivated?*
- *Do you constantly deal with fear in the form of anxiety, stress and worry?*
- *Does a lot relationship drama seem to follow you?*

If you answered *yes* to any of these questions, then welcome to the rest of the world! Everyone has to come to terms with how they process love and relationships.

DISCERNING A REJECTION MINDSET

Rejection has so many branches to its weedy root system, so it is important that we build our discernment. You may not experience every manifestation that is addressed above, but take note of the battles you relate to and let God reveal where He would like to heal and transform you.

On the next page is a more extensive list of patterns and behaviors that are influenced by a rejection mindset.

MANIFESTATIONS OF A REJECTION MINDSET

Insecurity

Identity Issues, Lack of identity

Performance Based Living

Constant Busyness

Identity confusion

Chronic Emotional Woundedness

Fear, Anxiety, Worry

Mental Illness Struggles

Relational Walls and Masks

Constant Relationship Separation

Twisted Communication

Relational Strife

Blaming

Relationship Sabotage

Constant Limitations in Life

Always Feeling Ignored/Overlooked

Bitterness, Resentment & Anger

A Hurt that Keeps Repeating

Discouragement/Depression

Feeling Separated from God/Others

Rejecting Others Before You Are

People Pleasing

False Responsibility

Excessive Striving & Overworking

Perfectionism

Excessive Neediness

Excessive Need for Validation

Excessive Attention Getting

Excessive Need for Affirmation

Envy and Jealousy

All Forms of Addictions

Condemnation

Religious Legalism

Feeling Like an Outsider

Guilt/Shame

Self-Pity

Victim Based Thinking

Hopelessness

A DISTORTED LENS

The way I often explain a rejection mindset is by putting on a pair of tinted glasses. Whatever shade those glasses have will be the filter by which I see everything in life. Rejection is a collective mindset and belief system. It wants to become the lens by which we view our world, affecting every aspect of our lives.

When you confront a rejection mindset and drive it out, your whole perspective on life can begin to change. Endless possibilities open up and needless drama no longer has a hold on your heart. You bring a more empowered self to relationships and are less prone to being taken out by the enemy's arrows.

QUESTIONS FOR CONSIDERATION

1. So far, where have you noticed that a rejection mindset has had an influence in your life?
2. Where do you find rejection interferes with your relationships?
3. On the list of manifestations, which words are issues that you see manifesting in your life?
4. What theme of rejection seems to follow you around?

PRAYER

Father God, I come to you in Jesus' name, and I thank you that there is an opportunity for me to delve further into love and healing. I am starting to see where rejection has had an influence in my life.

I need a deeper understanding of Your love and acceptance for me. I ask You to come and show me and help me to experience Your love. Help me break free of the deception that seeks to block me and hold me back.

I also ask that you reveal where rejection has become a way of thinking and a lens on my life, so that I can begin to take my freedom back. I want to stop experiencing a limited or defeated life.

Help me to have discernment, so that I am not blind to what is keeping me in bondage. I know you have freedom for me from rejection. I ask that You meet me as I expose rejection's lies and embrace Your truth that will set me free. In Jesus name, amen.

THE REJECTION MINDSET
IN ACTION

A rejection mindset does not form out of nowhere. It takes root within us through many challenging life experiences that become open doors for this toxic perspective. In my history of working with people, I have found that rejection often finds its way into our lives through ten main life circumstances.

1. *Your birth circumstances: unwanted pregnancy, birth order issues or being adopted.*
2. *Inherited rejection mindsets that run in your family.*
3. *Negative childhood experiences, like abandonment, neglect or performance-based pressure.*
4. *Father and mother wounds.*
5. *Traumatic experiences.*
6. *Physical, sexual, emotional and spiritual abuse.*
7. *Heartbreak and wounds during teen years.*
8. *Wounds from dysfunctional or unhealthy marriages.*

9. *Wounds experienced in the workplace.*

10. *Harsh words being spoken to you.*

The best way to see what a rejection mindset looks like is to walk through some case studies. These examples will give a picture of how this bondage keeps so many in a web of dysfunction and limitation. Rejection's deception can cover an entire gamut of destructive thinking and living. So, in reading through these case examples, take note of some of the patterns or mindsets that can manifest in your own your life.

DAN: THE STRUGGLE TO FEEL CLOSE TO GOD

For *Dan*, rejection has convinced him that God is far away, but he doesn't realize he's listening to lies. He feels that something is wrong with him that causes him to feel this distance from God.

This struggle is fueled by how rejection came into his life. Dan grew up with a father who was emotionally distant, so Dan also struggles with an up and down relationship with God. Intimacy with His Father in heaven is a constant nagging battle.

His daily cry is *"God I want to be close to You!"* Yet his battles continue to wage and he falls into silent discouragement. He feels that God's love for him changes from day to day, therefore he feels alone, neglected and on the outside of His favor. When he hears people talk about a growing intimacy with God, he crumbles even further, thinking, *"something must be wrong with me."*

REBECCA: NOT FEELING SAFE

In the life of Rebecca, rejection attacks areas of her life where she has not felt safe. Therefore, she always seems to have a looming anxiousness and nervousness. This has often led to battles with depression as well.

Growing up with alcoholic parents created an environment where she never felt protected and secure in areas of love. On top of all this, Rebecca beats herself up all the time, wondering why she can't seem to get over her struggles. She feels like she should be way further than she is and has a hard time realizing how her past has affected her. She looks at other people and wonders why she can't live like they appear to be. A rejection mindset trains her to daily beat herself up as to why she hasn't gotten free sooner.

PAUL: THE WEIGHT OF EXPECTATIONS

Paul is a pastor, who loves shepherding people and cares much about the life of those in his church. What he doesn't realize is that a rejection mindset forms a lot of his interactions with the people.

He's a constant people pleaser and works overtime to keep everyone happy. Meanwhile, the opinions of the people weigh on his shoulders. He's a workaholic and doesn't know how to turn off what is happening in the congregation. His wife and children are all aware that he is not emotionally present home. What happens at church dominates his mind.

They even see a different Paul when at home, because in church, he puts on a certain personality for people. Yet inside, there is a lack of personal joy and contentment in his life. He feels pressure to preach a certain way and doesn't have the freedom to just be himself. Meanwhile, his insecurities are leaking into his leadership team and affecting how the life of the church conducts itself.

BETHANY: A LACK OF ACCEPTANCE

For Bethany, rejection has blocked her sense of acceptance, value and belonging. She daily struggles in feeling comfortable in her own skin. She drifts in an endless search for peace and security. Because of the rejection mindset, she easily feels left out of relationships. When Bethany enters a room, she already feels like an outsider.

The biggest problem is that she doesn't understand that she is listening to lies. These thoughts play constantly and are so familiar, she knows of nothing else. No one taught her to discern her thoughts and feelings. So, the enemy speaks lies without ever being detected. At the end of the day, she believes these toxic perspectives are true, so her interactions are formed from this unhealthy foundation.

Exhausted from trying to fight these thoughts, Bethany has given over to saying, *"this is just the way that I am."* In the end, rejection has trained Bethany to believe that she is unwanted, does not fit in, is unloved, and even unlovable.

EDWARD: SOCIAL STRUGGLES AND AVOIDANCE

Because of deep insecurity, Edward feels very uncomfortable in social settings. So, he avoids them all together. You will rarely see him at parties, hangouts and small group settings. Besides going to and from work, he is typically alone and isolated. He will attend large group events like services at the large mega church in town. But one on one and small group interaction rarely ever happen.

His wife has become so frustrated and helpless with his social avoidance. She attends most events by herself, usually making excuses for why Edward is not in attendance.

Unfortunately, Edward hasn't recognized he has a broken heart, where rejection and fear have conditioned him to avoid people. Like many men who struggle with insecurity, Edward's idea of dealing with relational issues or challenges is to shy away from them. Rejection has driven him in fear into a quiet den of passivity.

HEIDI: OVERCOMPENSATING IN RELATIONSHIPS

Meanwhile, Edward's neighbor, Heidi goes in the opposite direction. While Edward isolates, Heidi aggressively overcompensates for her insecurities and rejection issues. Most would say she is *"over the top"* when it comes to relating.

Of course, Heidi fears being seen as weak and inferior, so she puts on a hyper-extraverted mask everywhere she goes. Her driving desire is to be known as the *"outgoing happy person,"* but deep inside, she's not at peace. On top of it all, she doesn't know how to just be herself. She tries way too hard and exhausts her energy. Sometimes her behaviors even turn people off, because she doesn't know how to relax and be real.

Heidi is convinced she has to keep this show going. She may over-talk in social settings or put on an *"everything is always great"* persona, so that no one will see her weaknesses and insecurities. Unfortunately, at the end of the day, no one knows the real Heidi.

MICHELLE: SEEING LIFE AS A VICTIM

Michelle can be a challenging person to interact with, as rejection has clouded her lens on almost everything. It trains her to feel that people don't love her and most are against her. Because of this, Michelle is easily embittered towards others and even God.

She carries a Rolodex of resentment, filled with reasons that validate why she can never catch a break in life. Rejection kicks up in almost every interaction, even in the mundane and simple day-to-day circumstances. When someone walks by her in the hallway and does not say hello, she wonders why they ignored her. There is an assumption that people are against her. She struggles with being hurt and offended, especially because she assumes the worst in people's motives.

Unfortunately, rejection has trained Michelle to live as a victim; life just happens to her and she will always get the short end of the stick. Walking into a crowded room, she often feels a sense of not fitting in. Most interactions are viewed negatively and Michelle can find herself accusing many people of being unloving.

The rejection mindset does not allow her to see that people actually love her or that she can be an overcomer. She is locked into a mentality that keeps her in a defeated lifestyle. She often thinks, *"Good things are not for me. The blessings of God are not for me."*

TED: SEARCHING FOR THE PERFECT WOMAN

Ted was burned by a woman he deeply loved. He longed for her affection and validation, so his life was crushed when she broke up with him. Rejection did a number on him as a result of his broken heart, making him deeply angry with women in general, never trusting them. So, he went from relationship to relationship, never settling down and committing.

Ted is searching for the perfect woman, but he never finds her, because his "perfectionistic" ideal does not exist. He is desperately searching for love, but is driven by infatuation. This lust initially propels him, but then quickly fades away.

Rarely can you get close to Ted. He gives you just enough to interact with, and then pulls back. Most people see that Ted struggles to give and receive true love. The fear is very evident in his life, but he's not willing to face it. Fear works as a megaphone in his thoughts. He responds to those thoughts quickly and as a result, never confronts his insecurities and pain. People around him try to love on him, but he is unable to receive it.

Ted can never seem to get over the female wound in his heart, but he has not understood that this wound runs deeper than just from a breakup. The deeper root system of pain in his life goes back to his earthly father, who was passive and his mother, who was verbally abusive and neglectful. These unhealed wounds have kept him from having healthy relationships with females.

DEANA: ATTRACTING THE WRONG MEN

Deana's rejection issues in her life drove her to look for love and validation anywhere she could find it. Whether it was spending endless hours at work, seeking to get affirmation from her boss or partying the night away, she was always driven by an excessive need to be loved.

Because of rejection's deep destruction in her heart, Deana always seemed to process life as an addict. When relating to men, she was attracted to those who were similar to the absent father in her life. They never treated her well, but she was attracted to them nonetheless.

She experienced abuse in her childhood and always seems to draw in the abusers in her life. Put her in a room with 100 men, where 99 are wholesome; somehow Deana will attract and pick the one abusive guy in the room.

ALAN: LUST AND ADDICTIONS

Her coworker, Alan had similar battles, where he could only relate to women from a place of sexual lust. Because of the rejection of his father and lack of nurture from his mother, he sought for women to give him the validation that he needed. Yet, his sexual encounters and pornography addictions never satisfied the longing in his heart to be loved.

Alan's thoughts were addictive and obsessive. He embraced most activities with an addictive mindset, approaching everything with an "all or nothing" mentality. Alan really struggled with being by himself, so he filled himself with busyness, so as not to face the pain and void in his heart.

HENRY: A LACK OF SELF-AWARENESS

Henry's validation issues are through the roof, so he overdoes it in almost every relationship setting. He is relationally needy but lacks the self-awareness to notice that he comes across in ways that make others feel awkward. He tries too hard in relationships and it causes them to withdraw.

Henry often speaks too much and doesn't know when to stop. He over-talks his resume and accomplishments. When you get into a conversation with Henry, you never know how to walk away because he just keeps talking. When you share something with him, he responds by going into his own story.

He rarely shows that he is listening, so it turns people off. Henry complains that he doesn't have any friends. But telling him that he may be a little "too much" in relationships or that he tries too hard, just makes him angry. He has little self-awareness as to how he comes across. He just can't see it.

BRENDA: THE NEED TO BE HEARD

A challenging wound in Brenda's heart is that she was never heard growing up. Her parents ignored her and downplayed her pain. In life, she often feels the pain of being ignored or unnoticed over and over again. She has even adjusted her life to the idea that no one really listens or cares anyway, so why bother.

Relationships can be very discouraging for Brenda, because she feels she has to do all the initiating. On top of it all, most of her attempts to reach out are ignored. Calls are not returned, texts are often unaddressed and it's very common for emails to have no reply.

The theme of being ignored seems to follow Brenda, to

the point that she gets used to it. She gets angry when people don't listen to her, so over the years, she has slowly stopped sharing. The current story she carries is *why bother, people don't care anyway.*

TOBY: RELATIONSHIP TWISTER

When it comes to conflict resolution, Toby is a very unsafe person. You can have wonderful interactions that are casual and on the surface. But get closer to him and you will find out how much of a skewed lens he has on people and the world around him. Whenever people get close, somehow he finds a way to sabotage the relationship by taking something the wrong way.

He gets easily offended and will create a story about how others are against him. Portraying a narrative of a martyr, every relationship story is filled with how wrong others have been to him. Yet when you see the common denominator in each story, Toby has never recognized his issues that have contributed to the fallouts.

Reasoning with Toby is almost impossible, because he doesn't hear what you are saying. He believes a twisted version of what is being said. Unfortunately, he has been at the center of a number of church splits and business fallouts, because his toxic lens infects every environment he enters. Until Toby realizes his own issues that contribute to the breakdowns, he will continue to blame everyone else.

BLOCKING THE POWER OF LOVE

Rejection bases its lies on painful experiences of the past or unloving environments that conditioned us to live by rejection's programming. When we are not settled in the power of love, we become prey to all manner of confusing and counterfeit ways of thinking.

All rejection needs to do it keep you from seeing how loved you are and keep you from manifesting that security in your life and relationships. Even if you are not being rejected, a rejection mindset will still convince you that you are.

QUESTIONS FOR CONSIDERATION

1. As you read through this chapter, which profile speaks to your battlegrounds the most? Why is that?
2. Which one of the profiles would be the toughest for you to have relationship with?
3. In the profile that you relate to the most, what is the major theme of struggle?
4. How have you seen that battle at work in your life?
5. What is one theme from a rejection mindset that you can begin facing and allowing God to heal?

PRAYER

Father God, I have seen some examples of what a rejection mindset can do in someone's life. Help me to discern how I have come into agreement with rejection and allowed it to fester in my relationships.

I want to live a more healed and free life, so open the eyes of my understanding, so that I may receive Your love and healing the way You meant for me to receive it.

I ask that as I gain recognition to what rejection has done, You give me the clarity and strength to walk in a renewed life. Thank You so much for Your love. I am grateful that I do not have to live with the lies of rejection. My past does not have to be my future. Thank You for Your love. In Jesus name, amen.

THE REJECTION CYCLE
OF LIMITATION

We all live according to certain beliefs and habits that create patterns in our lives. They become familiar ways of thinking and living that get passed down from generation to generation. Unfortunately, many of these patterns produce continual limitations in people's lives.

The very nature of a rejection mindset involves trapping a person and generations underneath certain limitations. They often don't even realize they are being held back, because it is all they know and are accustomed to.

At its very core, rejection seeks to separate us from our full potential. So, in the place of fruitfulness, it seeks to propagate limitation. It wants us to see ourselves from a limited identity, act from a limited perspective and manifest a limited journey. It will also condition us to get used to being a part of dysfunctional experiences. These limitations are very real and must be confronted to overcome the bonds that run in the family tree.

BREAKING OUT OF LIMITATION

Everyone has hardships, hindrances and limitations they have to face in life. Nothing is easy and each of us has our own areas to overcome. But we must be aware of what we are up against, otherwise we can find ourselves dwelling in the bondage of our history.

Many of our personal limitations involve where we came from, what we inherited and the agreements we make. Regardless of how they got there, it's imperative to see the spiritual war waging against us, seeking to prevent us from living in the fullness of love, fruitful relationships and a powerful impact.

Millions live underneath their God-given potential and destiny because of underground limitations that are at work within their life. Some discover them and break free, while others live continually under those limitations.

We can be confronted with limitations regarding relationships, influence, resources and more. Can you relate to experiencing certain limitations that seem to let you go only so far? Many people can relate to an invisible block that prevents them from a greater potential. This is a major work that rejection seeks to cultivate.

It is important to understand that a rejection mindset is always seeking to infect the root system of our lives and keep us bound by personal limitations. It will keep us under a cloud of limiting belief systems, programming us to think we can only go so far. Rejection wants to keep us in a holding pattern that never opens up and keeps us stuck.

CONFRONTING THE PATTERN

Most of my work with individuals involve helping them see the destructive cycles that work against their journey of living free. These cycles are like dominoes. All it takes is for one thought to engage and it sets in motion an entire series of patterns.

Once the toxic cycle is recognized, we can make a decision to interrupt that pattern and create a new one that is based on empowering perspectives. With humility, patience and intentionality, we can move forward to create a lineage of favor rather than limitation.

Here are the ten factors that create disempowering cycles that keep rejection-based results in our lives.

1. THE FAMILY TREE SETUP

Everyone is born with an initial family footprint. This involves patterns, ways of thinking and mindsets that run in the generations. Rejection mindsets run in most families in varying degrees. The experiences, perspectives and patterns have a deep inherited effect, right down to personality traits that can be based on rejection. This is especially true for rejection-based thinking that has not been eradicated, but often reinforced in how the family functions.

These mindsets that run in the family can include:

- *Sibling rivalries*
- *Unemotional interactions*
- *Certain relationship, business and ministry limitations*
- *Fatherless homes*

- *Unemotional mothers*
- *Addictions in family*.

This is what we often enter into the world carrying. There are certain limitations, where the family could only go so far in relationships, resources and influence. There are some caps that our ancestors never broke through for various reasons.

Everyone starts off with a certain amount of limitations. Rejection wants to keep us underneath those caps and to not move past those generational barriers.

Question: What family limitations were you born into?

---

2. HOME LIFE DYNAMICS

The family setup is reinforced through daily life, which enhances dysfunctional patterns. The rejection mindset becomes woven into the fabric of the generations. How the family members interact with each other, how problems are addressed and how emotions are dealt with become major components that can either set people up for breakthrough or a lifetime of struggles.

With most of the people I work with, they have family dynamics that keep them glued to their bondage. The moment they start walking free and paving a new path of freedom, a family member reacts in a way that pulls them out of their growth.

Guilt, shame and intimidation are often used to devalue the person's genuine attempts to walk into a healthier pathway. Being forced to keep family secrets or cover up the dysfunction can also leave many under the bondage. Here are some other examples of limiting family dynamics:

- *Family that doesn't talk about problems*
- *High levels of control*
- *Guilt-based interactions*
- *Performance based living*
- *Perfectionism*
- *Fear-based living*
- *Religious legalism*
- *Violent atmospheres and lots of anger.*

I often find that when someone decides to walk free from the family bondage, a barrage of guilt and accusation comes from family members. This is often used by the enemy to keep a person bound to old ways and prevent the new pattern from opening up.

Question: What unhealthy family patterns did you have in your home?

_____

_____

_____

_____

3. LIFE TRAUMAS AND DRAMAS

A trauma is a sudden negative life event that shocks our system to any degree. Everyone has a series of traumatic events they've experienced. They can become defining moments in a negative way if not healed properly. It's how we process and heal from trauma that makes all the difference.

I find a vast majority of traumas people experience are similar to what has occurred in their family tree. Strange patterns repeat and traumatic events often magnify the disempowering family dynamics.

For example, someone who grows up with legalistic religious parents can find themselves traumatized by a legalistic church that is spiritually abusive. A man who is ignored for promotions has a son who is experiencing the same problem at the same age. Somehow the damaged area of our hearts attracts traumatic events to keep us there.

- *Abuse of any kind*
- *Being ignored or neglected as a child*
- *Not being loved*
- *Events that communicate you are not loved or that you have to earn love*
- *A home life that was not safe*
- *Witnessing harm or violence*
- *Being fired*
- *Being falsely accused*
- *Near death experience*
- *Traumatic church experience*
- *Being ignored regarding talent, calling or gifting*
- *Father or mother passing away*
- *Teenage pressure, bullying, etc.*

It's been my observation that most people do not realize

how much their past pain affects their present struggles. We are wired to either mindlessly plow forward or remain paralyzed by the past. These events bury deep within us certain ways of thinking and belief systems that will hinder us in the long run if not addressed.

Question: What are some of the traumas in life that have affected you negatively?

_____

_____

_____

4. LIMITED THINKING AND BELIEFS

During low moments of pain, heartache and lack, rejection tempts us to come into agreement with disempowering thinking. It takes traumatic moments and negative experiences to validate that we are unloved, unworthy of love, unsafe, alone or a myriad of other disempowering thoughts.

Negative belief systems are often based on rejection and limit our ability to break free. These beliefs form the self-talk we listen to and the viewpoints that place a cap on our potential. If we are not careful, they can become the dominant narratives that we listen to all day long.

These rejection-based beliefs will cause you to see yourself and God from a tainted lens. In fact, the number one thing I see in people who recognize the trauma in their life is a sense of distance from God. They feel like God is far away and don't know what to do about it. Their bodies are stamped with the pain of the past. This is what rejection is all about.

Question: What are some of the limiting beliefs you carry about God, yourself and your life?

_____

_____

_____

5. SELF-PROTECTION

Without proper healing, we find ways to protect ourselves. The pain of past hurt, drama filled relationships and traumatic encounters are so strong, we do all we can to avoid them. In fact, most people spend their lives avoiding their past pain and moving to comfort as quickly as possible. Two main actions take place as we seek to self-protect.

a. We put up walls. It may be a mask you wear in relationships or a wall you put up to keep people at a distance. Sometimes chronic busyness will keep people from getting close to you. Vulnerability can the scariest thing in the world, because that could mean embarrassing exposure. So, we become unwilling to let our guards down, living as an emotional Fort Knox in the process.

B. We make vows. To protect ourselves, we make vows that are spoken out loud or rehearsed within our thoughts to keep us safe. They may provide temporary relief from pain, but they also keep us in a holding pattern. We may feel safe, but we never step into our full potential when holding onto these vows.

We are all called to take our pain, let God heal it and use it to bless others in a redemptive way. Yet our vows keep us

50

under a Plexiglas wall of limitation. People can't get to us and we can't get to them. This is a strategy of rejection.

Question: What are some vows you've made or walls you've put up to emotionally protect yourself?

---

6. A DISEMPOWERING STORY DEVELOPS

Point out your deepest struggles and limitations and you will also hear a story that seeks to verify them. Rejection teaches us to replay a story that validates our limitations. Instead of living out a story of healing and empowerment, we carry a narrative of limitation that justifies why we are where we are. It's one thing to recognize your history. It's an entirely different thing to remain there.

I've carried around many stories that were rejection-based. I even used Scriptures to back up my dysfunction. Many people have a locked and tight story as to why they are stuck where they are. It may have some facts to it, but it is also keeping them stuck.

We can easily blame the people in our lives. Blaming limitations on a lack of resources is a huge part of a disempowering story. Pointing to what other people have done to us is another common storyline. Sometimes, we can even use the story of "I am waiting on God" as a way to justify our victim posture. We are often waiting on God, while God is waiting for us to step up and believe a new story!

The problem we need to confront is the broken and disempowered story that plays on repeat continually. It sneaks into conversations, jumping in anytime someone asks a question. It is the invisible billboard people carry in their hearts. The disempowering story of hurt and limitation becomes the dominant narrative in the person's focus and perspective.

If you are ever going to change and breakthrough your limitations, you are going to have to be brave enough to identify your limiting story and confront the lies that are woven into it. Rejection wants to keep you there, but God wants to write a new story with you.

Question: What is the limiting story that repeats in your mind and discussions?

_____

_____

_____

7. THE STORY LOOKS TO BE VALIDATED

The limiting story looks for proof to back up its claims. This will cause you to look for patterns in your life that give evidence to rejection-based outcomes. So, you look for it. You will walk into a room with 100 people. Ninety-nine of them say nice things to you, but you pay attention to the one person who was rude.

Rejection always looks to be rejected and it will condition you to look out for any scent of rejection around you. It pollutes your focus, causing you to hone in on the negative and limiting factors, rather than seeing the opportunity of growth that you have before you right now.

If you are focused on a rejection mindset, you will find it. Whatever you seek out for, you will eventually find. If you look out for a limited life, you will find every reason and proof you need. Until the day comes when you change your story and develop a new focus in your life.

Question: In what ways do you anticipate rejection or a limited outcome?

---

8. REJECTION FOLLOWS YOU

One of the most bizarre patterns I've observed is how people attract situations that follow the broken themes of their past. Those who were ignored growing up are ignored by current interactions. Children raised by alcoholics are attracted to and marry alcoholics.

Even those who have been victimized—physically, sexually or verbally, often express that over time, they seem to attract predators in life. They find themselves in situations where people seem to repeat the same patterns against them. The rejection in them draws unhealthy people to them, keeping them bound and validating their perceived unworthiness, shame and lack of value.

There is no question we find ourselves being drawn to situations that match our internal belief system. People who don't love themselves will end up with people that verify that. Our internal thought world looks for connection. No matter what we say we want, our rejection hooks become a magnetic pull to keep the disempowering pattern going.

The ways of rejection will keep following you unless you face it and kick it out of your life. The same patterns that irritate you will follow you until the agreements are broken and new patterns are cultivated. This takes honesty and a real intentional walk of establishing new patterns of living.

Question: What are some dysfunctional circumstances that seem to find their way into your life over and over?

---

9. REJECTION SEEKS TO PROVE ITSELF TO YOU

There are two reports we can believe in any situation, what the enemy says or what God says. There is a great deal of difference between how God sees our lives, and how rejection, fear and all the junk of the enemy wants you to see it.

The enemy loves to use our past pain and heartache as leverage for what our future holds. That is why an unhealed past can affect us so deeply. If we ignore it, we can continue to repeat the cycles of limitation and not know why this keeps happening. Over time, rejection will train you to become used to these patterns.

After years of living in these cycles, we find ourselves in circumstances that hard wire us to believe we are stuck. These areas almost become untouchable for other people to speak into. The pain and heartache of situations have caved in, placing us in a posture of agreement with our limitations.

There are two dysfunctional responses to our painful past that many fall into. One is the response of striving. We put every cylinder into motion to make sure we don't remain in the bondage. Although it takes a great deal of consistent effort to move into freedom, people who hustle 24/7 don't often give room for healing. They easily burn out and crash trying to perform their way out.

Others see their rejection limitations and give up contending for more. They fall into agreement with a limited life. They assume a rejection-based future and surround themselves with verifiable proof that they can't break forward or change.

Question: What limiting beliefs do you find knocking on your door regularly?

_____

_____

_____

10. A VICTIM MINDSET KEEPS YOU STUCK

Rejection's ultimate mission is to make you a victim of your past pain and limitations. That negative resistance you feel when you try to break into new patterns is rejection seeking to keep you as a victim. It wears you out and keeps you feeling separated from God's empowering love.

A victim mindset will keep us separated from our empowered identity. It will also move us to a place where our limiting circumstances become our identity. Therefore, our relationship with God is based on the interactions with our unfavorable circumstances. We can't see above the storm because we've come under the power of what our limitations say to us. We become deeply ingrained as to why we cannot be free and move into a new life.

I see the victim mentality manifest the most in how people pray. Their posture is a *"God rescue me from this situation"* instead of *"God I know you are with me, you love me and there is a strategy for me to walk in freedom."*

Victims then ask very disempowering questions that keep them stuck. *"Why me?" "What did I do wrong?" "Why did I end up in this?"* Ask questions like that and you will be drawn to condemning and disempowering answers. Most people sabotage their prayers because they have no belief in what they are asking for anyway.

Victims then engage in a powerless relationship with God, asking Him to rescue them when He has already laid out the tools we need to overcome. Yet a victim is so focused on the story of bondage that he can't see the armor he's wearing that is capable of slaying rejection.

Therefore, this becomes the cap that gets handed off to the next generation. This continues until someone wakes up and says, *"It stops with me."* That person will need to get the healing necessary and carve a new pattern for future generations.

Question: Where do you find yourself thinking like a victim rather than an overcomer?

_____

_____

QUESTIONS FOR CONSIDERATION

1. When you look at your family tree, what is the biggest problem you notice coming from a rejection mindset?
2. How have people responded to pain in your family? Were they healthy? What changes can you make in how you respond to pain?
3. What limiting belief system keeps holding you back from your potential?
4. Do you have a vision of who you are and what you are capable of that is bigger than your current way of living?
5. What one step can you take today to create a new pattern for overcoming?

PRAYER

Father God, I thank You for illuminating the factors that contribute to limitations in my life. I recognize that my family tree has areas of blessing as well as limitation that I need to be aware of.

I ask that You help me to see the belief systems and mindsets that hold me back from experiencing Your love and living in my fullest potential. Grant me the courage and clarity to break through the hindrances that have held back my life and previous generations.

I take responsibility today as an overcomer. I choose life. I chose a new story. I make a decision to blaze a new trail of breakthrough, where new mindsets and new behaviors chart out a new legacy for people to walk in.

Forgive me for listening to a story that is not what You have given me. I choose to believe Your report.

I break agreement with rejection and the ways it keeps me in a limited cycle of living. I choose to stand on what You say about me and live it out. I thank You for it, in Jesus name, amen.

BEGINNING THE HEALING PROCESS

Here's the news you need to understand, so I will share it up front.

You have a broken heart.

Who me?

Yes, you.

Everyone, to some degree, has a broken heart, so stop denying or pretending it's not there. We live in a broken world, with broken people, who do not know how to love others properly. In addition, many have experienced the pain that arises when someone should have loved you, but did not.

We cannot address rejection only with thinking differently. We have to engage healing of the heart. If we do not place our focus on the health and life of our hearts, then we will waste our time in the transformation process.

When Jesus began His ministry, His first and primary focus was on the hearts of people, especially in bringing life and healing to the broken heart.

*The Spirit of the LORD is upon Me, Because He has anointed Me to preach the gospel to the poor; He has sent Me to heal the brokenhearted . . .*Luke 4:18a

Why focus so much on the heart? All of life flows from the heart and all transformation begins in the heart. Freedom from rejection is more than an attempt to "fix" your brain. It requires a receptivity to God's healing work in your heart.

THE BROKEN HEART EFFECT

The Scriptures speak about what happens to our spirituality when the heart is unhealed.

A merry heart makes a cheerful countenance: but by sorrow of the heart the spirit is broken. Proverbs 15:13

A broken heart can rob us of our health and allows sickness to run more rampant in our lives.

A merry heart doeth good like a medicine: but a broken spirit drieth the bones. Proverbs 17:22 (KJV)

How many times have we heard it said, *"She died of a broken heart."* Yet, how many people around us are slowly eroding from the inside out as a result of brokenness that has never been addressed or healed?

WHAT IS A BROKEN HEART?

We carry broken hearts because we were born into a world that does not know how to love us fully. When true love is missing, all kinds of hurtful experiences unfold. Odds are you have been the casualty of many. Yet even if you have not had a laundry list of painful experiences, you still have an emptiness that can only be filled through genuine love.

The problem is that no one helped you understand that you have a broken heart. You were told to just "get over it" or ignore there are any problems to begin with. But you knew all along that something was missing. It's the healing of your heart that has been waiting to happen all along.

Rejection takes a broken heart and fills it with lies that can stick for a long time. For all of us, the broken heart goes beyond friends, spouses and lovers; although they all may have wounded us. The greatest need for healing goes back to our relationship with our parents. The majority of our wounds stem back to these foundational relationships.

THE FATHER'S INFLUENCE

Both men and women need their fathers. Dads are designed to be the leading presence in the home, demonstrating the nature of Father God's love in the household. Because we live in generations where the father's presence has been absent emotionally and even physically, a deep wound has formed in hearts, perpetuating broken-hearted generations.

Fathers were designed to provide some very special blessings to the household; areas that rejection has stolen and counterfeited.

Loving Leadership. The wife and children were designed to thrive when the father operates as a loving presence in the home. His job is to be a leader, mainly by example, demonstrating the nature of God and His love in everyday life.

The number one mission of a father is not financial provider, though that is not to be neglected. His main role is one of a loving spiritual leader. His children need to experience his love. Too many people grow up saying, "*Well I'm sure my dad loved me. He didn't say it, but I know he did.*" This is a tragic example of what children are missing in the home while growing up.

Acceptance & Approval. The home needs the voice of the father's love, acceptance and approval. It must be spoken regularly. The daily life of the home was designed to be filled with his words that say:

- *I love you.*
- *You are a good son/daughter.*
- *I love you princess.*
- *I am proud of you.*

These are words sons and daughters ought to hear regularly. Dad's words are so empowering, allowing the children to soar to new heights. They can be free from unnecessary pressure, because acceptance and approval have already been established.

Covering. Any man who takes a position of healthy leadership establishes a blanket of covering to the household. They feel safe and protected in their journey, knowing that dad "has their back."

Identity. It is the father's job to tell you and show you who you are. Without the establishment of a proper identity, one will flounder back and forth in life without a steady rudder.

The majority of people on the planet have not experienced these blessings from their fathers. They have few to no memories of him saying the words, *"I love you."* He may have been a hard worker, but he was emotionally and spiritually passive in the home. This is the modern-day plague that the world needs healing from.

THE MOTHER'S NURTURE

One of the greatest powers a woman possesses is her ability to nurture. When this is not present, a child lacks the ability to comfort and encourage themselves. This is why addressing mother wounds is important, though they can be tricky to detect and address.

Nurture is the manifestation of love that brings comfort, coping and recovery from hard times. It restores our emotional capacity, especially after we go through a tough season. When you run outside and scrape your knee, who do you to go to? Mom. When you have a hard day, you run to mom because she was designed to tell you that everything is going to be okay.

God deposited a great deal of His nurture into the heart of the female. The mother brings an emotional component of nurture that satisfies, comforts and teaches us how to recover from the pain of life.

Those who have mother wounds lack nurture and often struggle to emotionally bounce back from hardship. They don't know how to comfort themselves and can easily struggle with moods swings. They can experience emotional instability, confusion and double-mindedness. Guilt will more easily plague them, and they will constantly struggle with being hard on themselves.

Battles of the mind can become a lot harder for those who had moms that were manipulative, cold or overly strict. They will lack the coping skills that nurture brings. Addictions will become an easy temptation for escaping pain. Eating disorders, smoking habits and pornography are common examples of addictions that stem from a lack of nurture.

The intention here is not to place blame, but to identify and recognize hindering wounds. It's an opportunity to stop wandering around aimlessly, wondering why we carry such deep pain from the battles and issues of the heart that cannot seem to be solved in a quick counseling session. These wounds formed us in many ways. Through this opportunity for recognition, God can get to the root of what is going in our life and lead us into freedom.

YOU'VE BEEN LEFT BEHIND: ABANDONMENT

Whenever mom or dad do not take their position in the home, rejection injects the poison of abandonment. The hurt of abandonment trains us in fear to avoid ever feeling that sting again.

Maybe your father left your mother and said, *"I'm never coming back."* You as a child feel all the repercussions of that and the impact follows you all through life. Though you may not be aware of it, you begin to see all your future relationships through the lens of abandonment.

"When is this person gonna leave me, too?" The rejection is constantly hitting you. Or, guilt may come in saying, *"It was my fault."* We can see how the actions, or lack thereof, of

those who were intended to love us, can create a lingering and pervasive negative spiritual climate within.

Those with unresolved abandonment issues always have a looming fear that people are going to leave them hanging. This also becomes transposed onto God, as though He will not be a faithful presence. Abandonment sufferers struggle to get close and remain close to people because they carry a fear they will be abandoned again.

JAMES' EXPERIENCE OF ABANDONMENT

Years ago, I was asked to speak at a retreat to a church group that was hungry for a move of God. The first night, I ministered on the Father's love and healing to the broken heart. At the end of the teaching, I asked those who wanted prayer on this issue of the Father's love to come forward. To my surprise, everyone rose up and moved forward to receive. Looking at the group standing before me, I was sobered as to how universal the father wound is.

What happened next was simply an amazing move of God's heart for the people present. As I slowly walked by, I spoke simple words into each person's heart. I stood in the gap for their pain and spoke words over them that they never heard. As their brother in Christ, I was fighting for healing of their wounds. Simple words like, *"I love you," "I am so glad that you were born," "I am sorry"* or *"You are a good son"* unleashed wells of tears as they experienced something they never received. It was a total leading of the Holy Spirit, touching the core of how God saw their past and pain.

One young man, James, took in my words, but was emotionless. He politely nodded, but I could tell my words were not penetrating his heart. He was probably the only one in the room who did not, from the outside, show a heart-felt connection to my words. I did not take this as discouragement, but as an opportunity to investigate. So, the following morning over breakfast, I sat down with James and asked him about his perspective of the previous night's encounter.

Before I tell you what he shared, let me inform you that James was a boy in his early teens who was morbidly obese. He seemed to carry a quiet sadness all the time. He was hungry for God, but you could tell there were some blocks in his ability to experience the love God was pouring out.

As he began to share his story, the first thing James said to me was, *"My dad told me he loved me all the time."* Hearing the words, *"I love you"* was not the problem. What brought deep pain and unresolved sorrow to James' heart was that his biological father never acted on those words. The phrase *"I love you"* actually became a cheap set of letters put together.

His father left when he was very little. In the process of separating from his mom, James' dad promised he would stop by and pick his boy up on a regular basis, so they could hang out together.

His father did not follow up on his word. He would promise to drive over and pick up James at noon on Saturday. Eleven forty-five would arrive and James would be at the steps, waiting with suitcase in hand. Noon would arrive and then pass by.

Twelve-fifteen would move by and mom would quietly

suggest, *"James, I don't think he's coming. Do you want to come inside?"*

"No. He said he's coming, so that means he's coming."

12:30, 1:00, 1:15, 1:30 . . . no sign of James' father.

"He's going to be here. He'll be here. I know he's coming," these thoughts raced through his mind.

As each car would appear and pass the house, his heart would jump, thinking his father was finally arriving. Instead, every car passing became a solid blow of rejection, abandonment and disappointment to his heart.

Meanwhile, James was developing a pretty serious eating disorder. He would hide chocolate bars under his pillow and regularly eat junk food as a way of comforting himself. His mom did the best she could, but his father wound was damaging his heart. His rejection wound of abandonment led him to find solace in what he ate.

Someone saying, "I love you" did not mean a thing to him. He needed to see and experience faithful love. When he didn't, he would resort to his reliable comfort--food. The Scripture in 1 John 3:18 comes to mind:

My little children, let us not love in word or in tongue, but in deed and in truth. 1 John 3:18

People need to see love, not just hear it. When words don't meet up with action, it leaves a confusing and deadly mark. Abandonment leaves people with a message that says, *no one is going to have your back in life. You're all alone in this.*

SOMEBODY LOVE ME: THE EMPTY VOID

One of the most difficult wounds to identify is the wound of lack. It's easy to see that physical abuse leaves a wound. Betrayal leaves a wound. When someone does something against you, it leaves a more obvious wound.

But it is very hard to realize that you carry a wound because of what you did NOT receive.

All your life, you should have been told you were loved. You should have been protected. You should have been nurtured. You should have been told who you are and what you are capable of. You should have received approval and validation.

When you don't know what you should have received, it's hard to even notice the brokenness. Those areas are numb and empty... a void gets left in the heart.

This void can create an excessive need to be loved that becomes an unending vacuum, sucking the life out of other people. We can also seek to fill the emptiness with counterfeit substitutes, mainly because **our fathers** did not fill that void with the love and affirmation we needed. You can try to comfort yourself with food, sex, or any number of addictions. The drug of choice does not matter, because rejection will train you to use it as a source of comfort and fulfillment.

That is why the workaholic, drug addict, overeater and porn addict, all have a similar thread of bondage. A void lies in their heart. No matter what you use as a substitute, the emptiness is never satisfied. This is why rejection can sometimes feel like a hurt that never heals, because there is a continual throbbing pain that never seems to get remedied.

I WILL NEVER: THE VOWS

A father creates a wound by his absence and his lack of engagement. From this pain, vows are made, a set of rules that we live by, a subconscious code on which we base every decision. Vows are constructed with terms such as "I will always" or "I will never." The danger in these vows lies in how we take them to others in our lives and how these absolutes never allow us a life of true freedom.[1]

When we are hurt, the temptation is to protect ourselves. Vows give us a sense of validation for the protective walls we put up. With vows, our emotional barriers become more solidified in our hearts. We then live with barriers to keep dangerous people at a distance. When in reality, we end up keeping *everyone* away. Yet over time, what was once a wall for protection becomes a prison we are now enclosed in.

A rejection mindset propels us to make vows. It is not uncommon for people to make major declarations like,

- *"I'll show them!"*
- *"I'll prove them all wrong!"*
- *"They'll regret not loving me."*

These vows can actually prevent us from being able to engage people with a vulnerable heart. We end up walking through life with unreasonably heavy armor on. Here are some more common vows declared from wounded hearts:

- *"I will never be hurt again!"*

---

[1] From the documentary movie, Absent: absentmovie.com

69

- *"I will never let this happen again!"*
- *"I will never be married again!"*
- *"I will never trust a woman."*
- *"I will never cry."*
- *"I will always have to do this all on my own."*

In order to be released from our vows, we have to be willing to process through the pain we are avoiding. We live in a culture that avoids pain at any cost, so building walls and making vows in our hearts is very easy to do.

THE DETACHED HEART

The detached heart is the inability to emotionally connect or empathize. Someone with a detached heart can go through the motions of working, raising children and going to church. In our culture of busyness, you can get away with little heart connection, but over time, it will catch up to you.

When rejection runs deep within a person, the heart can become so disconnected that a "shutdown" mechanism comes into play. They only know of "going through the motions" in life.

When a heart is alive and awake, we have the ability to access pain as well as enjoyment. Even though life is tough, a heart that is alive works through healing and has a sense of hope and excitement. People with detached hearts have not been trained on being vulnerable and how to process pain.

Living without connection to life's events, they become calloused over time. With a heart that is detached, there becomes hardness and heaviness. It's torturous to be around them because they do not respond to problems with genuine empathy or action. They often sit passively. On top of it all, they have a stubbornness that is not ready to change. They become lethargic to any personal renovations that require heart-connected effort.

A detached heart can make transformation incredibly difficult. People in this scenario can often be the most challenging to minister to, mainly because they want God to come down and just remove all their junk and make them feel alive again. In addition, no amount of preaching, teaching or exhortation will move them unless their heart gets stirred to action. A person with a detached heart needs to make a powerful decision to move into a whole new direction of thinking and living.

QUESTIONS FOR CONSIDERATION

1. In what ways are you seeing that love was compromised in your life?
2. Is it easy for you to see where you have a broken heart? If so, take some time to consider how that has affected you.
3. Take some time to consider the father wound. In what ways do you carry this in your life?
4. Take some time to consider the mother wound in your life. In what ways have you been able to observe the effects of this?
5. What is a wound you can give to God for healing today?
6. What one action step can you take to move into a healthier direction?

PRAYER

Father God, I come to You in Jesus' name, and I thank You that You love me. I ask that you begin to show me where my heart is broken. Come with Your love and heal me in the areas where I do not know Your love.

Bring me to a new level of recognition where rejection has sought to pollute my life with its lies and deceptions. Give me the courage to face the hurt in my heart and allow You to come in with Your mighty love. I want to tear down the walls of my heart, but I need to see where those walls are. Set me free from the ignorance I may have to the bondage that is in my life.

Renew my heart with Your love and fill those empty places with Your love. You are a Father to the fatherless, so I invite You to come and heal my father wounds. Where my mother may have struggled to nurture me, come with Your comfort and balm of healing to bring rest to my heart. I love You Father God, help me to know You as my Dad. In Jesus' name. Amen.

FEELING FAR FROM GOD

As human beings, we were designed to walk in fulfilling relationships. Unfortunately, so many are unfulfilled and even emotionally starving when it comes to their connections. On top of this, many feel very disconnected from God.

One of the top heartaches I witness in the lives of believers, if they are honest, is the struggle they have in connecting to God. In just about every scenario, I find rejection at work behind the scenes to keep people bound in this frustration.

THE ASSIGNMENT OF SEPARATION

I have spent a large amount of time working with people who have had incredibly painful experiences in life. Their ability to maintain emotional health was incredibly challenging during these negative seasons. I noticed the pain was further compounded by a sense of distance they felt with God. When they needed God the most, they often felt separated from Him.

Many do not know how to press into God's love for healing. Most have never been taught. Therefore, rejection hovers over their painful situation, sending messages that disempower their connection to the Father and hinder the healing that is available in Him. The top lies rejection perpetuates are *"You are far from God," "God has left you hanging,"* and *"God is not here."*

Feeling a sense of separation from God is the easiest way to identify rejection's lies in our thoughts. That is because the very nature of rejection is to cultivate a sense of distance in relationship. The enemy knows what these feelings of separation will do and the domino effect it will have on every area of our life. Therefore, the adversary works intentionally to ambush us with rejection to keep us in this prison.

WHY DO I FEEL SO FAR?

As a believer growing up, I felt far from God all the time. Rejection conditioned me to feel that way. I would ask, *"Why am I far from you God?"* My question was based on the lies I believed.

When we believe that God is far away, we come into agreement with rejection. Then the enemy follows up with a series of accusations as to why God seems far away. *You feel far because you don't read your Bible enough. You haven't fasted. You don't pray enough. You had a lustful thought today. You were lazy and didn't get anything accomplished. You are not worth being loved. You are far because something's wrong with you.*

This would lead me into a tailspin of repeated and

unproductive repentance. I don't even want to call it repentance, because it involved confession based on lies. The story rejection tells us is that that God is far away, when in reality, He is very near.

The problem was not God. The problem was not even me. Something was in the way. Rejection was working overtime to keep a veil over my heart. It spewed continual lies that kept my heart from knowing that my loving Father accepted me, just as I am. I didn't need to perform for Him or achieve some kind of religious perfectionism to connect to His presence. But for years, rejection had disempowered my ability to rest in the eternal love of God.

THE ROOT PROBLEM

So, in order to heal this issue, we need to get to the root problem. The struggles with our Heavenly Father go back to our relationship with our earthly father. Whatever theme of frustration you seem to have with God is often the narrative you carry from your earthly father relationship. We learn to relate to God by how we related to our earthly father.

When listening for God's voice, we have been trained to tune into the voice that sounds most like our Dad's. If we have not been loved properly by our fathers, rejection trains us to hear a voice that is counterfeit to God's, even though we may think it's God. Therefore, over time, we place the attributes of our earthly father onto God.

Rejection seeks to make us feel separated from God and follows up with a painful list of reasons. This can lead us to blame our struggles and frustrations on God, as though He left us hanging. Satan knows if he can make God the reason or source for our pain, there will be a continued sense of separation from His love.

The world is full of people who are very angry with God. They have been mistreated and unloved, where God's nature has been misrepresented. A skewed view of God develops while rejection continues to foster separation from God's love. The pain of life gets projected onto God; as though He was the author of it or He left during a great time of need.

THE FATHER IMAGE

Rejection keeps us from feeling safe in relating to God as our Father. Many believers are comfortable interacting with Jesus, praying to Jesus and calling out to Jesus, yet they carry a discomfort in having relationship with Father God.

I was one of those people. Because of the rejection strongholds in my life, I was very uncomfortable interacting with Father God, especially in the dimension of addressing Him as *Abba* or *Dad*. I felt like it was sacrilegious to address God as *Father*, or even *Dad*. I preferred to just talk to Jesus.

There is nothing wrong with calling out to Jesus, but there is a deeper dimension of relating to the Godhead. The Scriptures unanimously teach that our prayer and connection is ultimately meant to lead us to the Father. We are to pray to the Father in the name of Jesus. Jesus is the *way* to the Father. We cannot have a relationship with the Father apart from Christ. At the same time, Jesus did not die on the cross so we would only know Him, but that we would also know the Father.

Jesus took the sting of rejection on the cross so that you

and I could freely interact with our Heavenly Dad. The cross and resurrection made it possible for you and I to connect to that great love and to know who we are as the Father's children. Jesus knew what it meant to carry the sins of the world and feel separation from the Father on the cross. He took that upon Himself so you and I would never have to feel separated from God. Rejection contradicts this truth and trains us to live in continual feelings of separation.

GO TO THE FATHER

Jesus said it Himself in addressing our prayer relationship with Father God. Before ascending to heaven, there would be a new order for the body of Christ to pray. Because of Jesus, we do not need someone to go to the Father for us. We can go and talk to the Father ourselves.

And in that day, you will ask Me nothing. Most assuredly, I say to you, whatever you ask the Father in My name He will give you. Until now you have asked nothing in My name. Ask, and you will receive, that your joy may be full. John 16:23-24

Let me push this even further. Jesus is also not going to pray to the Father for you.

In that day, you will ask in My name, and I do not say to you that I shall pray the Father for you. John 16:26

Jesus was basically saying, *When I ascend, you will not ask Me for your needs; go to the Father. Go in My name. That's your access. Go to the top level and ask the Father everything you need. And by the way, don't think that I am going to say this prayer for you. I won't do this for you. I paved the way so you can know Dad yourself.*

In what is known as the Lord's Prayer, Jesus taught us to pray, *"Our Father."* All the New Testament Scriptures teach us how to have a deep relationship with Father God through Jesus Christ. Jesus came to show us the Father and lead us to Him.

As believers, we are the betrothed bride of Christ, but we are also sons and daughters of our Father. If we do not have an ingrained understanding of a love relationship with Father God, then rejection will build a blockage in our hearts and keep us from becoming immersed in the security of love.

Despite this truth, I have observed that the majority of believers I met today are crying out to Jesus while avoiding the Father. The rejection wounds of their heart have blocked them from this great privilege of connecting with Abba. Unfortunately, they will continue to avoid this issue until the father wounds of their life are addressed and healed.

During an incredibly intense moment in the garden, Jesus spoke intimately to Father God by using the word *Abba*, which means *Dad*. The strength that empowered Jesus to the cross was fueled by a secure relationship with Abba.

And He said, "Abba, Father, all things are possible for You. Take this cup away from Me; nevertheless, not what I will, but what You will." Mark 14:36

Even though God will not leave us or cast us aside, rejection teaches us that He will. It will even use religious ways of thinking to make us feel unqualified to be near God. This is how deep the work of the enemy is in seeking to keep us from the love of our Heavenly Father. If Satan can keep you convinced that you are far from God, He has disconnected you from experiencing the most important relationship in your life.

The father wound is certainly a major place where healing is needed. But in order to become healed from rejection, we cannot simply run to our earthly father and ask for his approval. This will lead to further disappointment and bondage. If you carry a father wound, your dad does not know how to give you what you need anyway. This leads us to turn where the solution lies; our heavenly Father. He is the only perfect Dad.

KEY TO FREEDOM

Letting God heal our broken heart will begin to remove the tentacles of rejection from our lives, so that we can pursue love relationships the way God intended us to. Admitting this shows you are willing to authentically address a core issue your heart longs for. It pushes past any pride or stubbornness that would keep you from being made whole and lets the One who loves you pour His goodness deep into your heart.

QUESTIONS FOR CONSIDERATION:

1. Talk about your experience with God's love. How do you experience it? Do you experience it at all?
2. Where have you noticed that rejection is working to make you feel separated from God and His love?
3. How has a rejection mindset taught you to feel God's love? (Perform, Get Busy, Perfectionism, etc.)
4. In what ways have you avoided the Father and only connected with Jesus?

5. In what way can you allow God to heal the father wound in your heart so that you can safely connect to Him as Father?

PRAYER

Father God, I recognize that I struggle in my life to feel close to You. I also struggle to receive Your love and experience it in my heart. So today, I give You permission to come and heal my broken heart. I give You permission to heal the father wounds in my life and show me who You are as a good Father.

You are a good Father; I just need to experience it more in my heart. Thank You for Your patience and kindness. You love me and I know You want to have a great relationship with me. Today I receive that. I make a decision to receive Your love as you heal my heart and set me on a new course. I am Your beloved child. Thank You for being a good Father and for loving me. In Jesus name, amen.

HEALING OUR INSECURITIES

An identity crisis looms over our culture. Masses of people are living with little idea of who they are and what they are capable of. They have settled with a lesser identity than what God says is possible. Insecurity has even become a way of life, unless we learn there is more available.

If you boil it down simply, insecurity is at the root of all relational breakdowns. Unhealed insecurity can leak into any community and pollute the health of connection. It will prevent anyone from living out your true God given identity. Insecurity can be described from multiple angles:

- Uncertain: *not confident or sure, deficient in assurance*
- Unsafe: *not adequately guarded or sustained*
- Shaky: *not firmly fastened or fixed*
- Instability: *not highly stable or well-adjusted*

Insecurity is a sign of emptiness, revealing that a person has not been affirmed and filled with a solid awareness of who they are. If those empty places are not fathered and nurtured, a rejection mindset forms, keeping us living in unhealthy patterns.

So, we are left with two choices. Face our insecurities so that God can heal us, or hide and defend them at all costs. The decision you make in this area will determine how much transformation you will experience.

When insecurity rises up, do you act on it and defend it, or do you use those moments to become more aware of your need to be healed? Unfortunately, too many invest more time and energy covering up and defending their insecurities. Meanwhile, the enemy uses that ground as a pivot point to form all kinds of toxic behaviors.

BROKEN OUTLETS

Insecurity leads us into two common patterns. In the first, we can carry an inward hostility, where our unhealed heart manifests anger. It's a violent combustion that can be subtle or overt. Anytime an insecurity is touched, anger jumps forward to defend and protect a felt deficiency. Men often do this, simply because we do not like to be seen as weak or incapable. We may use anger to control and dominate situations, making other people the problem so we do not have to deal with what is going on inside ourselves.

We can also give into a socially acceptable form of hostility — *performance and drivenness*. We overcompensate for our insecurities by chasing achievement, to earn approval and validation from others. We strive to make others happy and fill our days with constant busyness. This leads us to constantly compare ourselves to others to alleviate our insecurities.

The second extreme we can swing towards is withdrawal and emotional passivity. We let life happen to us and allow other people to make the decisions. A passive husband, for example, allows his wife to carry the load of daily decisions, making her the initiator and leader in the home. This keeps a man locked in a spiritual slumber that prevents him from confronting his insecurities. Passivity will manifest to keep a person from being moved to action.

Sometimes we can bounce back and forth between these two extremes because we have not been centered in who we are. We end up becoming stressed out on one end; running, running, hurry, hurry, going, going, and going! Burnt out, stressed out, and often with nothing left to give. After time, we crash, exhausted, saying, *Forget it!*" We then stray over to the other side into passivity, forfeiting any semblance of initiative, saying, "*No one really cares anyway!*" This is the life of insecurity that keeps us from a stable daily pattern of living.

INSECURITY REVEALED

God will work through our lives no matter how insecure we are. That's how good His grace is. Yet if we do not allow Him to develop our inner life, then insecurity will sabotage our long-term effectiveness. What our giftedness draws in can get shipwrecked by unaddressed insecurity.

I believe the time is ripe for us to confront our insecurities in a more aggressive manner. True works of God are often squelched because insecurity rises in the camp. God is working in ways to lovingly reveal insecurities, granting us an opportunity to heal. We will face the same problems over and over until we deal with the insecurity that prevents us from breaking free.

THE INVITATION OF ADVERSITY

Those who overcome insecurity view challenges in life as an invitation to grow into maturity. Meanwhile, others will defend, blame and complain, while remaining in the status quo. All the while, dysfunctional patterns will continue to manifest.

Those who have made the decision to live as overcomers, use adversity as an incubator to face their insecurities and grow. They do not waste energy hiding weakness or brokenness; they plunge into the learning that is available. This is the power of growing into sonship and out of spiritual slavery. We lay down a rejection mindset that avoids facing insecurity and instead say, *"God, I receive my sonship. Today, I am Your son and I receive that. I choose to face the insecurity of my life and allow You to heal me. In my most challenging of seasons, I choose to grow."*

PERSONAL INSECURITY FACED

The struggles of my life led me to a place of decision. *What was I going to do with my insecurity?* During my younger single years, a battle followed me in relationships, one that involved the fear of commitment. I had a deep fear of intimacy, but didn't know it for a long time. Relationships with females were really challenging. Many men struggle with a fear of commitment, but I was deeply tormented.

Watching so many failed marriages and my own brokenness created a terrifying wall in my heart. The very thought of marriage and long-term commitment would send me into panic and unrelenting anxiety.

For years, insecurity made it hard for me to gain any sense of peace in committed decisions. Eventually the fear began to move into every area of my life. The fear infected my decisions for hiring staff, signing a lease on an apartment or even a two-year cell phone commitment. As silly as it may seem to some, I know what it's like first hand to be confronted with my insecurities.

For years I covered up these issues. Like many, I defended my ways to concerned friends and mentors, even using certain Scriptures out of context to justify my dysfunctional patterns. I was a professional at over-spiritualizing my distorted reasoning. Meanwhile, the years of avoiding these insecurities were taking a toll, but I had no idea how to face them and heal. It took a hard realization that if I continued in these patterns, I would end up alone and deep into mental illness.

I was left with a decision: mask over the fears and insecurities, justify them or allow God to do surgery on my heart. This is where bravery comes into action. Most people ignore the signals of insecurity and cover them up, rather than allowing God to take them on a journey of discovering who they really are. Being brave doesn't mean you have no fear. It just simply means you are willing to go somewhere fear doesn't want you to go.

STOP DEFENDING IT

The only way I began to experience freedom was when I stopped defending my insecurities and positioned myself to face them and be healed. I had to allow healthy people to mentor me, speak into those areas and hold me to a better way of living. Otherwise, my defensiveness would become a stubbornness; blocking me from the greater life I could experience.

We are all in process. The quicker we can admit to this, the more room we will give to ourselves and others to heal and grow into becoming more confident in our identity. I find that we are all playing the same game of hide and seek. We want to be found, but we spend our lives hiding in our insecurities.

When you are defensive in relationships and "put up your dukes" in conversation; those are often the areas where humility and vulnerability need to take shape. As you become less defensive, you will be able to discern what may be hindering you with greater clarity. You will not be as blindsided because there's nothing to ignore or hide. We grow the most when everything is in the light for God to have access.

1. Become more comfortable with vulnerability. Living vulnerably can be scary, but each step you take to lower your guard in healthy ways will help you connect to your identity with greater clarity. Everyone around you craves vulnerable and authentic interactions, but someone has to take the first step. Without it, you imprison the power of who you really are.

2. Stop comparing yourself to others. The moment you feel bad about yourself, the enemy will convince you to look at others. Comparison only increases the voice of insecurity and can be the number one "joy-thief" in people's lives. There is no healing in measuring our worth in comparison to someone else.

How often do you find your thoughts looking to comparison as a gauge in life? How does this prevent you from living your life to the fullest? How does holding up the standard of being like someone else diminish the unique person that God created you to be?

QUESTIONS FOR CONSIDERATION

1. In what area are you waiting for someone else or something else to make you feel secure, when you need to dive into God for that?
2. Of the reasons that keep insecurity intact, which one is an area you need to face and begin to walk free from?
3. Where do you need to stop comparing yourself to other people?
4. In what way can you begin living more authentically and vulnerably in relationships?
5. What battleground reveals your insecurity? How can you begin facing it with a different perspective?

PRAYER

Father God, You are an amazing Father, and I come to You, because I can be secure in You, through Christ Jesus. I ask that You reveal Your love to me. Your love provides the security that my heart desires. I make a decision to trust You more and take a stance for my security in You. Help me to confront the areas that

I have ignored or pushed away and give me the understanding to walk in greater security. I do not want to live with insecurity being a driving force in my life any longer.

Today I make a decision to stop hiding my insecurity, but to give it over to You in Your love. I am only truly secure in You, so I choose to let my heart receive the healing I need so that I can stand securely in who You made me to be.

I choose to live vulnerably and with more authenticity, so that others can receive the courage to do the same. There is also no reason for me to compare myself to anybody else, because You have made me with a unique, special and powerful identity. Tell me who I am and grant me the grace to grab a hold of that identity. I thank You for that. I receive it in Jesus' name, amen.

REBUILDING YOUR IDENTITY

W hen did you find out who you really are? If so, who was the person most responsible for communicating that to you?

Most people have no answer to either of these questions. That is because identity is meant to be spoken, confirmed and validated from those in our tribe. It should begin with our parents and be reinforced by our particular circle of overseers. Very few have memories of being told who they are, which is why insecurity runs so ramped. It leaves our hearts open to enemy attack all the time.

YOU NEED TO HEAR WHO YOU ARE

Identity security is best reinforced through verbal affirmation. Those who play crucial roles in our life are meant to utilize significant moments to speak and affirm blessing over who God made us to be. Words are critical during key transitions in life, where at each stage of growing up, we receive equipping that guides us into the next stage.

Very few initiations exist in our modern society. The best western culture can offer are the stages of getting a license to drive, being old enough to vote in elections and arriving at the age to drink alcohol. Not an impressive list.

Therefore, most people are left to leap out and figure out life 100% on their own with little to no understanding of who they are. Instead of building their future upon the foundation of an affirmed identity, they wander through life in survival mode.

A NEEDED EXPERIENCE

Even our Lord Jesus needed to have His identity spoken and affirmed. His example sets the template that our tribes need to follow. Before officially launching His ministry, Jesus went to be baptized. It was at this event where His identity was verbally affirmed by the Father.

When God the Father spoke, He used the occasion, not to place the spotlight on Himself, but to affirm His Son. One sentence summarizes what every human heart needs to hear, *"This is My Beloved Son, in whom I'm well pleased."* (Matthew 3:17)

All who were present had the opportunity of bearing witness to the divine exchange in this declaration: *"This is my Son! I love Him! I am pleased with Him! I approve Him!"*

These words are what every person on the planet need to hear over and over again. You need to know who you are. You need to know you are loved. You need to know you are approved.

Growing up, our dads are the ones assigned to initiate this process. Without our earthly father's identity affirmation, we are left to flounder in the storms of life. The enemy's work festers when there is little identity validation set in place.

One of the greatest responsibilities of a parent is to equip their children to maximize the power of who they are. In the countless consultations I have sat in, the majority of people who struggle in life were never equipped, spiritually, emotionally and practically for life. They were not given the love they needed, nor were they given tools to overcome. Too many families are setting up their children for failure, because they are not affirming and equipping God's identity on their child's life.

SECURE TO OVERCOME

Receiving love, approval and validation from His Father empowered Jesus to enter the wilderness and face temptation from the devil. What the Father established in Jesus, Satan immediately challenged: "*If you are the Son of God. . . If you really are who you say you are . . .*"

The devil wanted to see if Jesus was truly secure in who He was. If He had been insecure, or had rejection in His life, He could have easily been swayed by the temptations that were thrown His way. Yet our Lord's response flowed confidently from identity. "*It is written!*" was not just what He did, but who He was. (Matthew 4) He was and is the walking, talking Word of God and calls us to live in the same manner.

Jesus needed to hear the love and approval from His

Father, to imbed identity into His being. You cannot learn identity in a classroom. It must be imparted through a fathering relationship. Otherwise we will only know in theory who we are, yet struggle to demonstrate it.

WHO AM I?

Jesus taught the power of identity to Peter by asking a simple question.

But who do you say that I am? Matthew 16:15

Peter astounds Jesus with his response.

You are the Christ, the Son of the living God. Matthew 16:16

Wow Peter! You got it! Only divine revelation could have shown Peter the true identity of Jesus. His response was not based on man-made criteria. He didn't get this from reading the papers. Others had put a label on Jesus, saying He was a good teacher, rabbi or prophet. Peter got the download that was so much more accurate.

Our Lord quickly turned this moment to call out Peter's identity, which means *rock*; exhorting him in his identity as a "rock" for the body of Christ.

And I also say to you that you are Peter, and on this rock I will build My church, and the gates of Hades shall not prevail against it. Matthew 16:18

Jesus refers to Peter as "a rock," yet he did not manifest a secure "rock" identity right away. The affirmation of identity did not dismiss Peter from the battles he would need to face. Much like you and I, he had his season of stumbling to manifest his identity. I bet when Peter stood before the people on the day of Pentecost and preached with boldness, this exhortation of Jesus in Matthew 16 came back to mind.

GETTING A REVELATION OF WHO I AM

My willingness to let God heal me opened my heart for some divine encounters with truth. I remember an experience I had while driving in my car years ago, where I felt God speak to my true identity. It was a season of transition and preparation for new things. I was facing my insecurities and giving God permission to heal my heart.

As I drove, I had been meditating on the subject of identity and was rehearsing some of what I felt God was saying about me. I still had lots of fears hovering over me, but I was hungry for breakthrough.

In a moment, it was like God interrupted my thoughts and a faith filled vision flooded my heart. For a moment, the internal chatter of insecurity halted and I was able to see who I really was and what I was created to be. God did not talk to me about my insecurity. Instead, He pointed me to the bigger picture of who I really am. This is often how He deals with our junk, by simply reminding us of who we are.

Immediately, I sensed God bringing attention to my name *Mark*, which means *"mighty warrior."* From there, I felt a flood of thoughts fill my heart of what it looked like to live as a mighty warrior for God. Not only did this give me the courage to break through my fear and insecurities, it created a domino effect in my life where I began to face all my circumstances with greater boldness.

Mark, you are a Mighty Warrior of Jesus. It is your name and it is who you are. You are a front-line warrior. I'm going to use you to touch all kinds of people. You are a warrior, a mighty warrior who will show people how to connect to their hearts. You are going to lead an army of overcomers who will passionately know the love of the Father and walk in delivering freedom. This will all arise out of you understanding who you are.

I began to weep because I was so overwhelmed by the love and confidence I felt from my Father. Ever since then, I've made the tough decision to face my insecurities and walk through whatever I need to, so that I may experience the healing my heart needs. It all started when I became more tenacious about coming into agreement with who God made me to be while taking massive action in a way that aligns with that identity.

Many things in my life shifted when I decided to stop toying around with insecurity and step boldly into what God says is possible. The potential for my life was incredible, but I had to come into agreement with it and start taking my stand against what made me insecure. From that moment on, I knew the power of the Kingdom of God would grow in my life as I took that posture each day.

I had to come to the place of saying, *"Father, I'm going to believe You and what You say about me. I'm going to step into who You say that I am as a dearly loved son and stop letting this insecurity keep me in slavery."* Since then, I have made it a commitment to daily rehearse my identity so that it becomes imbedded into my DNA. Growing in identity security takes time, but the more I practice who I really am and shed who I am not, the more I land in confidence.

REBUILDING YOUR IDENTITY

Over the years, I have encouraged others to be aware of some specific mindsets. In order to detox from the insecurity that holds us back, here is what I have found to be helpful.

1. Start breaking Agreement with Who You Are NOT. I often teach people who they are NOT, to help them understand who they really are, because we often tolerate and live in agreement with ways that are getting in the way. Many are not even able to hear who they really are because they carry too much interference that blocks them from receiving it.

Much of who we are has been formed by insecurity, rejection and fear, leading us to try to be someone that we are not. This keep us from freedom involved in simply living as God's child.

2. Disconnect Your Identity from Your Performance. If we are to break through our rejection mindsets, we need to know that who we are is not based on our performance. A stable identity cannot be based solely on how much achievement we attain, success we have or how perfect we do things.

Many people link their roles as being their identity. Those roles include being a spouse, parent and whatever we do for work. Even though they represent areas of responsibilities, they do not define our core identity. **At the end of the day, who you are is a child of Father God. As a believer, you are a son. You are a daughter.** Connecting to sonship is the key to breaking the back of insecurity.

3. Begin Documenting who God Says You Are. This is the

most practical step, because you need to develop a focus to retrain your heart on how you see yourself. It involves writing down and declaring who you are on a regular basis.

I recommend that you find powerful Scriptures and write down a list of personal identity declarations. Make it specific and personal. Rehearse them by declaring them out loud on a daily basis. Practice this in real time, because no one ever arrives in one moment. It takes regular practice and reinforcement from people around you who can affirm your God-given identity.

4. *Get Around People Who are Growing in Who THEY Are*. If you want to enhance who you are, get around people that will sharpen you and affirm your unique identity. Find people who will speak to you not as you are right now, but who you are becoming. Create a loving and nurturing environment where people are encouraged to see themselves in a greater light than they are currently living by. Determine today that you will cultivate a safe environment for people to overcome their insecurities and step into greatness.

5. *Take Action*. I need to live by who God says that I am. This often comes down to my decisions and places in life where I need to take action. Passivity will only keep us living according to the old identity, along with all the junk that comes with it. Only by taking action can we see our new identity begin to manifest in greater power.

We build our identity through practice. We cannot expect some prayer moment to lift this completely off. We also cannot wait to feel better before we take action.

Stepping forward goes hand in hand with overcoming the insecurity.

Sometimes it comes down to a simple choice that will engage the powerful identity you carry. What choice do you need to make to move into agreement with who you really are?

QUESTIONS FOR CONSIDERATION

1. Think about the identity that you manifest. What things, good and bad, seem to show forth?
2. Did your father speak his love and approval to help establish your security?
3. What do you wish your father would have said to you?
4. Where did you get your identity from?
5. Take a moment to think about what God says about you. Who does God say that you are? Write this down and keep it in a place where you can review it regularly.
6. How can you begin to affirm the identity of other people around you?

PRAYER

Father God, I thank You, that You have given me a divine identity. I recognize that there are things in the way that keep from living in connection to who You say that I am. There are fears, insecurities and other mindsets that have gotten in the way.

I'm grateful that you love me so much as Your child. Thank You for being patient with me, because Your grace will help me see who I am and act on it. I want to stand firm in who You say that I am.

I ask that You speak to me and let Your word ring true in my heart. I want my identity to line up with what You say and not what my brokenness or the enemy says. I want to stand firm into who I am in Christ Jesus.

Please help me hear Your affirmation, validation and love over my heart. I do not have to live in spiritual slavery nor do I have to be bound to my insecurities. I can live firmly in the new identity. Show me who I am in Christ and empower me to manifest it powerfully. I thank You for this opportunity. I receive it in Jesus name, amen.

THE FEAR OF REJECTION

For years, I would walk into a room with a sense of discomfort that would keep me uneasy. Fears were driving my thoughts, but I often didn't know what to do with them. *What are these people gonna say to me? Are they safe? Will they accept me? Am I gonna get hurt by someone?*

Most people engage relationships with a lot of fear-based self-talk going on. Some are so aware of it they don't even bother interacting with others. Others overcompensate with busyness, over-talking and relational masks. Honestly, we all try to put on our best, but deep inside, there is a tension we carry into relationship interactions.

It's all about having confidence. Yet the problem is, you and I were not given much equipping to walk around with true relational confidence. Very few have a *"Clint Eastwood in western movie"* type confidence. We're more often like Napoleon Dynamite giving a speech or fumbling to get through conversations.

The point is, fear is more present in our thoughts than we often admit. Insert a few unpleasant or painful interactions with people and we're imprinted with a loop of fear's voice nagging us all day long.

TAG TEAM ASSAULT

The rejection mindset uses fear as a driving presence. Rejection enters wherever there is pain or heartbreak. Fear enters to make sure it never happens again.

We all have fear issues we need to face, but so many are still neck deep in the river called Denial. They are blind to their own fear issues. They may say,

- *Oh, no Mark, I don't have fear in my life. I am just really cautious.*
- *I don't have fear. I am just concerned.*
- *This is not fear. I am just worried.*
- *This isn't fear. I am just stressed out.*

We often find ways to avoid facing the reality that we are afraid. Most all, we are afraid of being rejected.

A MOTIVATING PRESENCE

Fear can be an intense motivator. Its voice is loud and often obnoxious. Yet at the same time, it can operate quietly with deception. It will use whatever tactic it can to lure you into listening to its ways.

In certain settings, fear can serve us to avoid getting hit by a car or to run from an animal. The problem is, most people are not running from animals on a daily basis. Yet we can be prone to fear's voice all day long.

Those who are honest can admit many of the choices they make are influenced by fear. It drives us to make frantic decisions or at times avoid doing anything at all. If we are not discerning to the ways of fear, it will continue to drive us and dominate who we are.

FEAR IS A TERRORIST

The top priority of fear is to steal our peace and confidence. It keeps us in torment and holds us back from moving forward with boldness. The Scriptures tell us the nature of fear, showing us that *"fear has torment."* (1 John 4:18) The very nature of fear is torment, comparable to the work of a bully or a terrorist.

The greatest effect that terrorism has is intimidation caused by the threat of impending doom. The projections of the future become filled with darkness, negativity and dread. Fear works as a terrorist by locking down your ability to see the future through faith, hope and love. It will create a narrow focus for you based on what you hope will never happen. As long as you let that dread-filled scenario occupy your attention, fear has you in its grip.

THE DEMANDS OF FEAR BASED THINKING

When fear speaks, it demands that we pay attention, so that it can fulfill its wishes in our lives., including:

- *Immobilizing us or keeping us in a passive posture, so that we do not make decisions and take action.*
- *Developing a narrow focus on our hurts and what we hope will not happen.*
- *Creating a story of our future with a negative outcome.*
- *Taking past hurt and transposing it onto everyone we meet.*

- *Creating a paranoia in relationships, where we develop a view that people are out to get us.*
- *Running from pain and into comfort as quickly as possible.*
- *Living in the constant "buzz" of stress-filled days and hyper-busy schedules.*
- *Exhausting our energy and keeping us from living refreshed.*
- *Living from a place of daily pressure.*
- *Training us to become controlling.*
- *Driving us to make panic decisions.*
- *Stealing the joy of the moment.*
- *Focusing on the next event and not being present.*
- *Robbing us of our peace, so that we can never settle.*
- *Stealing the power of boldness.*

ADDRESSING OUR SENSE OF SAFETY

Both fear and rejection seek to separate you from living in and experiencing the safety, security and power of the love of God. Love is really the answer, but fear is determined to keep you from resting in this freeing love.

Our world of relationships works best when we feel safe in love. Feeling disconnected from love can be the most frightening place on earth. The deception of rejection is that we can feel unsafe even when the room is full of love and safety.

AVOID OR GEAR UP

Under this tension, our physiology will engage a *fight or flight* response. It's the body's messaging signal to deal with any situation that does not feel safe. It was designed to help us survive during a temporary crisis; like lifting a heavy object off someone or evading a bear in the woods. The

102

problem is most people are not running from a bear in the woods. They are running from their past pain and living in apprehension over their present circumstances.

The *fight* aspect of fight or flight is the response where we gear up, strive and become hyper driven. It involves performance-based living, perfectionism, people pleasing and constant busyness. All these traits are ways to overcompensate for our lack of feeling personally safe. The stress response of *flight* is when we get away from any danger. This is how people avoid situations that could pose any potential threat. Any level of danger in life can loom over our mind for days, weeks and even years.

EXPERIENCING LOVE

God loves perfectly every time and His love is the antidote to fear. When we learn to receive God's amazing love for us, fear no longer has a place to hold on to.

There is no fear in love; but perfect love casts out fear, because fear involves torment. But he who fears has not been made perfect in love. 1 John 4:18

Love comes from God, but it also must be experienced in relationship with our brothers and sisters. Each interaction ought to give us a demonstration of love. Yet this is challenging for so many of us that have been damaged in relationships. The hurt and pain of life drives us in rejection to withdraw from others or wear a mask.

WHERE YOU NEED LOVE THE MOST

Show me your deepest fear and I will show you where you need love the most. Your fear battles reveal where you have not been loved. Wherever fear is, love is absent. Love needs to come in to displace fear.

The Scripture reminds us that *perfect love casts out fear*. Defeating fear occurs best through experiencing an environment of love. Solid love cannot be built in one prayer session, but over time. It takes a process of building healthy relational exchanges that imprint love in our hearts.

When John writes, "love *casts* out fear," it is the same language used when Jesus cast out an evil spirit. Love is gentle towards you, yet violent towards the enemy. The formation of God's love within us has the power to drive out fear.

THE SPIRITUAL FORCE OF FEAR

For God has not given us a spirit of fear, but of power and of love and of a sound mind. 2 Timothy 1:7

Thoughts have an origin and are not always our own. We could be hearing a thought from God or from the enemy. It takes discernment to know the difference. When God speaks it often sounds like our own inner dialogue. But at the same time, we can be listening to thoughts and impressions of fear, without realizing it.

Fear is a spiritual force and must be discerned when evaluating our thoughts. Satan knows if you are not discerning, you will think fear is just your own thinking.

Fear has an intelligence that seeks to condition us in fear-based thinking. We can discern fear's presence by noticing the thoughts we allow. If you are good at identifying fearful thoughts and feelings, you can discern fear's voice.

NOT OF GOD

Tormenting fear does not come from God. He did not create you to live in long term, chronic fear of any kind. His desire is to deliver you from all your fears and confidently set your feet on His solid rock.

Some people are deceived so much by fear they think God is using fear to tell them something. They believe the panic or anxiety they are experiencing is a sign from God. I bought that lie for so many years of my life. I thought if fear was coming my way, then it was God speaking to me.

Years of peace were stolen from me, where I could have walked with such freedom, but was boxed in, chained by every whim of fear. I did not see it at the time, but I was trapped in a life that was unfruitful. I thank God for His love, grace and mercy, but like many others, I had to get rewired, so I could perceive the voice of God.

God does not use tormenting fear to teach you something. Why would God give you something that He has said in His word He does not give, but in fact, desires to set you free from? Sometimes just clarifying the battleground can give you so much more leverage for victory.

FACING FEAR

So how do we start gaining freedom? Here are some action steps to begin with:

1. Honestly recognize where fear has an influence. If possible, do this with a close friend. We cannot get free from fear if we are justifying it by saying, *"I'm just a worry wart," "This is isn't fear, it's just deep concern"* or *"I just don't like getting close to people."*

2. Recognize the need for your heart to be filled with the love of God. Any area that struggles with fear is an area that has not been strengthened in love. A true revelation of the love of God is what will drive out fear more than anything else. We often need to begin by recognizing our broken heart and letting God do a healing work to the wounds that lie within.

3. Begin to have value for healthy relationships. People who are motivated by fear can end up going into hiding because they have been hurt so much. But we need healthy relationships if we want to be whole. Many do not have close relationships because of past wounds and fear. Yet we must step out and face fear by being ourselves and connecting with others.

God will often use the people around you as relational laboratories for you to grow in how you see yourself and your relationships. If you don't value growing in relationship, you will not see any need to admit or even address the subject of fear. Yet at the end of the day, we must understand that God values relationship. He wants us to be whole with Him, and also with each other.

4. Write down the specific fears you face and break agreement with them. Be specific. Fear is not something to be argued with. It needs to be renounced. Otherwise you will keep tolerating its torment in your life. Start simply by saying out loud, *Today I break agreement with the fear of* _____. *I renounce its ways from my life.*

5. Face your fears and let the walls come down. I know

this takes time, but at some point, we have to take the leap and give it a try. Trust again. Open up again. The worst thing about having walls is that we end up living in a prison. My goal is to see God heal you so that you can get back out there and live without being chained to what dangers you think might be out there.

QUESTIONS FOR CONSIDERATION:

1. In what ways are you noticing fear gets in the way of fruitful relationships? How has fear held you back from what is possible in your life?
2. What are the themes of fear that seems to pop up in your life the most? If you don't know, ask God to show you.
3. In what areas do you need to let God and others love on you?
4. What is one step you can take today to face your fear and begin moving in a new direction?

PRAYER

Father God, I come before You in the name of Jesus. I thank You, that when I come to You, You can deliver me of my fear. Right now, I take responsibility for fear in my life. I recognize where it has been at work. I do not want to be ignorant of it any longer and I don't want to defend it anymore.

I break agreement with fear, including stress, anxiety, panic, worry, phobias and dread. I lay my fears down before You today, God. I repent and renounce of allowing fear to be a motivating presence in my life, where it holds me back from what is possible.

I take a stand against fear in the name of Jesus. Fear, I renounce your ways and I will no longer tolerate you in my life. I bring the cross of Jesus Christ against you and take my place as a child of

God, who is loved and cared for. I will no longer tolerate fear as a friend in my life. I command all works of fear to be removed from my life. I command fear to leave in the name of the Lord Jesus Christ.

Father, help me experience Your perfect love. May it drive fear out of my life. I receive Your perfect love, the kind of love that casts out fear. I say "yes" to it today. I want a revelation of Your love for me. I want to know love to the point that fear no longer has a grip on me.

I ask right now that You touch my heart with a deep experience of Your love. Perfect me in Your love and deliver me from my fears. I make a decision today to step into Your peace and walk in the rest You have for me. Thank You for loving me so much. I am so grateful to who You are as a loving Father. In Jesus' name. Amen.

THE MASKS WE WEAR

A s a child, I remember the fun involved in wearing a costume. Dressing up as an army soldier or a rough and tough cowboy was something my imagination could run wild with.

For children, there is little need for extravagant material for costumes. A simple bandanna over my face and a wooden stick for a gun was all the material I needed to pretend I was the toughest sheriff in town. I loved putting mud on my face and crawling through the woods, imagining I was serving in the infantry, ambushing the enemy in the name of freedom.

Whether it was a superman cape or a cheesy plastic mask, we all loved the idea of dressing up as someone. Children love to play dress up. Even adults participate in what are known as masquerade balls; lavish parties where masks are adorned to conceal the real identity of attendees. The costume and mask gave each person the ability to roam through the party without anyone recognizing their true identity.

Although these parties were designed for fun, in real life, masquerades have become an emotional protection for many. It's the number one way people seek to protect themselves.

THE MASKS WE WEAR

Masks are the most common way we put up walls in relationships. It's a fabricated version of ourselves. It is not the real us, but a constructed personality. There are a variety of masks we wear that can change depending on the environment. It all depends on what we lean on to feel safe or validated in life. Here are some ones that people wear:

- *The Happy Person:* no matter what, they are always projecting happiness, even when it doesn't seem authentic or applicable to the moment.
- *The Funny Person:* always has a joke or something to laugh at. You know it's a mask when it is time to talk about something serious and they have to always make a joke.
- *The Professional Person:* always in that role; can often take themselves and what they do too seriously.
- *I Have It All Together Person:* never seems to show weakness or vulnerability.
- *The Spiritual Person:* always has a scripture to say and always appears to be very deep.

Social media has become the perfect place to don a mask. In fact, it can reveal the lack of depth in our relationships, because they are all based on an image that is projected. Many use this opportunity to post a fabricated life that lacks any authenticity or reality. This only adds to the loneliness and lack of depth people experience.

Most of the masks people wear involve being trapped in their roles. A role is a responsibility we have, but it is not our core identity. Your core identity is not a mom, dad, worker, pastor or business professional. Your identity is God's child. Yet if you are not deeply connected to that, you will easily find yourself immersed into a role as a core source of identity affirmation.

THE PRISON

It is completely acceptable to have healthy guards and boundaries when it comes to relationships. For many, however, healthy, everyday guards have become thick walls that keep *anyone* from ever seeing their hearts.

We end up believing the walls are a fortress to keep us strong, when in reality, they are the lining to what has become a prison cell of bondage. In reality, masks keep others from seeing that our hearts are broken, discouraged, lonely and aching for healing.

We've been trained to put up walls to the extent that no one knows the real us. We need to start asking, "*Can the real you please show up?*" Yet many have no idea how to get out of their masks, because they have lived with them for so long. Presenting a false self has become automatic. Discovering who they really are can seem awkward at first, yet it is also a great tragedy when you live as someone who is not the real you.

God does not call us to just survive, He wants us to live abundantly and freely. Yet the only way we can truly live free is to begin to confront our walls. We have to be willing to put the mask down.

GETTING TO THE *"WHY"*

We love it when other people are real and authentic. Our eyes well up in tears and our hearts flood open when someone is vulnerable and shares their heart. We are actually drawn to those who let their guard down and share their real self. At the same time, however, we still go back to the enemy's bag of tricks and put on our masks. Why is this?

1. We Were Not Loved and Nurtured in our True Identity. The biggest reason we do not live in the freedom of our true self and wear a mask is that we were not affirmed and equipped to live in who we really are. It often goes back to childhood or young adult years, where a mask got strapped onto us that we have been wearing ever since.

2. We Do Not Like Who We Are. A big reason why we fabricate and live like posers is because we do not truly like who we really are. Therefore, many have lived their entire life wanting to be someone else. Whenever we do not love, accept and cherish who God created us to be, we often form ourselves into someone we think people will like. We mimic their mannerisms or develop their idiosyncrasies, hoping we can impress the world as they do. Yet, during all this, we are rejecting the beauty of who we really are and the significance of our unique blueprint.

3. The Fear of Exposure. The thought that fear perpetuates is that others will find out who you really are inside, which can be incredibly scary. It can be terrifying to think they may see that you are not always who you say you are. As human beings, we hate to see our weaknesses exposed. We show our strengths and celebrate them, but keep the weak parts behind closed doors.

We all long for authenticity, but we have to remember that authenticity means that *what you see is what you get.* You don't pretend to be something that you're not. This does not mean you wear all your problems and weaknesses for the world to see, but it does mean you are not going out of your way to hide them. You are also not one person to a certain group and a different person to another group.

The Scriptures tell us what living inauthentic lives are compared to: *Fervent lips with a wicked heart are like earthenware covered with silver dross. He who hates, disguises it with his lips, and lays up deceit within himself.* (Proverbs 26:23-24)

Talk is cheap, but a mask can make it even cheaper. One of the greatest tragedies is found in a person who is lost and in need, but is still pretending and putting on a facade. The lie underneath goes like this, *"If I let you get really close, then you will see the real me, with my flaws and weaknesses. And I am afraid you won't like it and reject me."*

4. The Fear of Rejection. The lie that drives the fear of rejection is, *"If I show you who I really am, and you don't like me, that's all I've got and its tough luck for me. I don't have a 'plan B' person I can pull out of a hat."* Who do you fear rejection from the most? The list usually involves those who have the greatest influence over your life. This starts with parents and branches off to friends, teachers, coaches and bosses. The person, whose approval you want the most is often the one you are afraid of being rejected by the most.

5. The Fear of Being Hurt Again. Fear teaches us to keep people at a distance, so as not to experience the past hurt ever again. People often avoid deeper fellowship because they don't want to be exposed and hurt again. But when we avoid authentic fellowship, we lose the environment of true freedom. That is not living at all, but barely even existing. So, the question for you today is, *"What will you do with your past hurt?"*

6. The Fear of Being Seen as an Imposter. This involves the fear of being exposed for something you are not. Many feel like a hypocrite, because they are helping others, yet struggling with many of the same struggles everyone else has. They feel accused, like they have to "arrive" before they can ever be qualified to help others. This makes them feel like an imposter. In the process, they are often driven to cover up these weak areas.

GOD DOES NOT ANOINT MASKS

In a culture that admires flashy power and impressive charisma, we must be reminded that God does not anoint masks or fabricated walls. He anoints the real you! The problem is that most of us do not even know who the real "you" is! That is why it is so important to move from fabrication to authenticity as soon as possible. The longer you delay this, the longer you will struggle to know your beautiful and God-given design.

God loves it when you get real with Him. You can't lie to Him so quit trying. In addition, He wants you to learn to stop lying to your brothers and sisters around you. They see your masks anyway, so go ahead and pull the protective walls down.

God uses you most when you are just yourself. This may not be flashy or land on web site headlines, but who you really are moves the winds of heaven, when you connect to it. God not only uses us in our weaknesses, He loves it when we don't try to hide them. He loves using the real you!

REMOVING THE MASK

Here are some applications to take to heart, if you are ready to let the guard down and allow God to heal you.

1. Face your fear by becoming vulnerable. One of the biggest steps that disempowers the tentacles of rejection is removing the mask. We can let it down by saying, "*You know what? I'm just going to be me, because my Father in heaven loves me, and He's made me in His image. He accepts me right now. So that's what I'm really going to show.*" This does not give us license to act disrespectfully or rebellious towards others. But it does involves coming to peace with yourself, weakness and all, living out the treasure of who you are.

2. Step out into the light and get real. You will have to do this one step at a time with people who you can build trust with gradually. Your freedom depends on you moving into the light of authenticity and transparency. God will deal with any issue you bring to Him, simply let go of the mask and come out of hiding.

But if we walk in the light as He is in the light, we have fellowship with one another, and the blood of Jesus Christ His Son cleanses us from all sin. 1 John 1:7

3. *Find someone you can be real with.* Start with one person. James 5:16 tells us to *"confess your trespasses to one another, and pray for one another, that you may be healed."* The most powerful dimension of God's power takes place in the arena of authentic connection. Yet this does not arrive without work and investment. Building a culture that values authentic heart connection will welcome the healing power of God.

4. *Learn to make what God thinks the most important voice.* Psalms 56:11 says, *"In God I have put my trust; I will not be afraid. What can man do to me?"* Studies have shown that our self-esteem is based on what we think the most important person in our life thinks about us. As believers, if we make God our Father this person, then what He says about us will become the compass of who we are and what our value is. His love is endless and will release you to feel safe in who you are, even though you have not arrived yet.

A major problem is that what people think has become an idol to us. Fear makes it seem like their approval is the most important thing in the world. Our self-esteem and worth too often rests on what people say and how they feel about us. Yet when we drop our masks, relax, and just be ourselves, we become released from the pressure of what people think we need to be.

Remember what Jesus said: *"If you lose your life for My sake you'll find it"* (Matthew 10:39). When we really address that fear we say, *"You know what? I'm taking a step out in faith; I'm just going to give my life over to Jesus Christ and trust that God is going to work in my life!"* It is there we will find our safety and security. As awkward as it can be sometimes, will you have the courage to face the masks you wear, so you can let down your guard and allow God to do a real work in your heart?

QUESTIONS FOR CONSIDERATION:

1. It is totally healthy to have proper boundaries and guard over our hearts, but where in your life have your boundaries become a deep wall, where people do not have access to the real you?
2. Which mask mentioned do you relate to the most? You may even share one that was not mentioned.
3. In the reasons listed as to why people wear masks, which ones do you connect to the most?
4. What would your world look like if you and those close to you were able to live without a mask?
5. In what way can you become a safe place for people to let down their masks?

PRAYER

Father God, thank You for loving me and accepting me, where I can be safe and secure with You. I recognize that it is not always easy to let our walls down, so I ask You to help me. I want to be more real and I want to have real relationships. I ask that You help me face my hurt and face fear, so that I can let down my walls and be free to be myself. Let me be one who can encourage others to be themselves, so their hearts can be touched for Your glory. I thank you for this, in Jesus' name. Amen.

11

THE SLAVERY OF REJECTION

I remember one day in prayer, feeling a declaration rising up in my heart. Words were stirring up inside as I was ungluing myself from a rejection mindset. I found myself saying out loud with conviction, *"I am not a slave. I am a son!"* A major shift in overcoming rejection was taking shape, as I took my stand against the spiritual slavery that kept me from apprehending a life of sonship. I was shaking off a bondage that I know had been in my generations for centuries.

Breaking free from a rejection mindset will involve tearing off the shackles of spiritual slavery. Rejection pushes us and seeks to keep us in its chains. If we are not aware, it's tactics will continue to grip us, while never allowing us to maximize the potential of spiritual sonship.

The Apostle Paul had to remind the church, saying, *you are no longer a slave but a son, and if a son, then an heir of God through Christ* (Galatians 4:7).

How many people have not accessed their true inheritance as heirs of God because spiritual slavery kept them imprisoned? Everything can change when a person breaks free of spiritual slavery. But keep in mind, you can leave the circumstances of bondage, yet still carry the mindsets of it with you. Israel was called out of the slavery of Egypt, yet they struggled to let go of the mindsets that slavery imprinted on them. Leaving spiritual slavery can be very challenging when it is all that we know. So it is important that we recognize there is a much better way that God has made available to us.

A FAMILY NOT AN ORPHANAGE

With spiritual slavery in the midst, people live more like orphans than family members. Too often the church looks and operates more like an orphanage than a healthy growing family. On top of this, there are too many unhealed orphans leading the church in the ways of rejection and keeping people bound in spiritual slavery.

With God, we are never left as orphans. But rejection will fight this truth, using your painful experiences to keep you from feeling accepted into God's family. The enemy wants you to have very little sense of belonging and an empty connection to identity. This will make it much easier to keep you wandering without a clear sense of purpose.

God has offered us an invitation to leave spiritual slavery and embrace sonship through Christ. But just because you are a Christian does not mean you have left the ways of spiritual slavery. Those who have embraced sonship have learned to receive this loving grace that connects us to the Father.

A son does not earn his place in the family; he is born into it. That is why the picture of entering the Kingdom of God is shown as being *"born again."* We have to restart what it means to be sons and daughters of a loving Father.

THE DISTORTED LENS OF SPIRITUAL SLAVERY

Rejection fights this invitation by keeping us in spiritual slavery, which will distort how we see ourselves, others and God. A slave feels distant from the Father, while sons always know they are close to the Father and know He is always available.

Rejection seeks to keep us in a negative pattern of disempowering experiences that we never rise above. Whatever the negative storyline, rejection wants to keep the patterns repeating so that our actions and behaviors continue in this viscous cycle. We all have to confront the resistance of this battle if we are to break free from spiritual slavery and move into the sonship available to us.

Here are seven key characteristics of spiritual slavery.

1. A SLAVE'S IDENTITY IS BASED ON PERFORMANCE.

Most of the burned-out people that come to my office have lived as spiritual slaves their whole life. They focused their attention on performing and getting approval for what they did, but were not equipped to live in sonship.

The only way spiritual slaves know to pursue intimacy with God is through constant activity, which drives them on an emotional roller coaster. One day they feel somewhat close to God and the next far away. Their way of evaluating themselves is based on their performance.

Because a slave lacks understanding of who they are, the first temptation is to find an identity in what they *do*. They immerse themselves into doing things to earn the approval of others and feel a sense of worth.

The constant doing and striving will not lead to peace and will keep you stuck in a continual restlessness that never ceases. Everything you do throughout the day will carry a pressure, where your identity, self-worth and value are based on how well you perform.

The identity of a son is based on who he is--a son to his Father in heaven. He has gratefully received this sonship and stewards it confidently. A son is content in who God has made him to be, so performance pressure is not a driving force.

It's hard to develop healthy intimacy with those caught in spiritual slavery, because they are always focused on their work more than connection. You may see them perform great feats or accomplish outstanding results, but you'll struggle to ever get close to them. They serve tables, but they don't know how to sit at the tables. Their ability to connect does not go beyond their roles of service. Take them out of what they do and they don't know how to function.

2. SLAVES LIVE WITH A SCARCITY MINDSET.

Because they lack vision, slaves always see life from a place of survival. Their eyesight focuses on the lack and not the possibilities, therefore, impossibilities dominate their thinking. Scarcity from past conditions train them to fear failure, poverty and lack. Impossibilities cloud their thinking in what God can do. They even wonder if God is working in their life and are unsure if He will show up to help.

Sons are very mindful of their inheritance through Christ, so they think from a perspective of abundance. They are filled with gratitude and are tuned into what God is doing. They serve a God who is *"more than enough"* and trust that in life's journey, God will meet them and show Himself faithful. While slaves are stuck in "scarcity" or thinking based on lack, sons live from a place of supply and abundance, knowing that God has more than enough to establish every good work in their life.

Sons are rooted in the love and goodness of God, and life does not deter them from deepening their understanding of this. They will be challenged in many areas, but their core stance in God's goodness is not removed. This is because they have experienced the love of God and it has become a compass for their heart.

3. SLAVES STRUGGLE WITH UNCONDITIONAL LOVE.

Spiritual slaves lack a foundational understanding of love and a revelation of grace and mercy in their life. As a result, rule-keeping becomes their only reference for relationships. They approach God from a place of trying to obey all the rules.

This also applies in relationship with others, as slaves cannot view people through the eyes of unconditional love. This is because they have not received it. So, they conduct earthly relationships with black and white rules. They tend to keep score in relationships, focusing on who is right and who is wrong. There is little grace, mercy and forgiveness in this dynamic. Ultimately, their slave-based relationship with God flows into all their earthly relationships.

When spiritual slaves read the Bible, they translate it according to the letter of the law, rather than the spirit of the law. They take passages out of context and hold others to rules and regulations in a legalistic manner.

Sons don't ignore the rules of life, they just don't make them the foundation for having relationship. Sons carry the love of the Father in their hearts, so they live from a place of connection with Him that flows towards others. Sons want to know the heart of God more than just jotting down a list of rules to live by.

4. SLAVES BECOME VICTIM TO CIRCUMSTANCES.

Spiritual slaves are constantly looking for an external force to take them out of their circumstances and save them. Failing to be rescued, a slave's circumstances begin to control them. They become ruled by their negative experiences. The struggles they encounter dictate their attitude and decisions.

As a result, spiritual slaves can become very negative and hopeless in their outlook. They can even lose value in maintaining integrity, so living with solid character becomes less important. They become discontented and ungrateful in the way they view things, and hard times become more fuel for their lousy perspective on life.

Spiritual sonship, however, is really about learning to grow up and understand that we are strengthened through hardship. Sons learn to mature in the hardest of times and rise up above circumstances, because of what has changed inside of them. Sons have embraced what has been provided by Christ and are daily activating and living it out. They always know they have a choice in how they respond to what happens in life.

A son is never controlled by his surroundings. In fact, sons will use seasons of turbulence as critical opportunities to be creative and find brilliant solutions. Some of the best in who we are as sons can come out through the most difficult of circumstances.

Slaves want situations changed, rather than being changed themselves. They often want the easier way in life. Therefore, they live underneath challenges rather than above them. Sons use the hardships of life as an incubator to grow and experience the greatest transformation. Slaves always focus on circumstances changing, while sons can grow up in ANY circumstance.

5. SLAVES FOCUS MORE ON COVERING UP THAN LIVING VULNERABLY.

Spiritual slaves are deeply insecure, mainly because a father figure did not affirm their identity and potential. Nor did he reinforce love in their hearts. Most spiritual slaves have worked for slaves and have been led by slaves their whole life.

Because of the performance world slaves are raised in, they seek to keep the image preserved. So, they protect and hide weakness and insecurities. Sons, on the other hand, have learned to rely on the love that God has for them.

Spiritual fathers have imparted a sense of security, so that the fear of failure and vulnerability does not torment them. Sons know they are approved no matter what, so it frees them to live without those fears. When mistakes arise, they use those times to learn and grow, not collapse. Sons are not preoccupied with making mistakes or worrying about what other people think.

Sons live their destiny *out* of their identity. Slaves try to find an identity by *pursuing* a destiny. Do you see the difference? Slaves are more concerned about where they are going. Sons are more focused on letting God build up who they are becoming; therefore, allowing their destiny to flow out of their identity.

6. SLAVES LIVE IN RELIGIOUS STRIVING.

The basis of a relationship with God for spiritual slaves is their religious striving. They cannot feel any peace unless they pray enough, read the Bible enough or engage in religious service enough. There is a driving force to please God rather than living from the goodness of God that has already been given in His love and grace.

Slaves constantly battle unworthiness, never truly loving and accepting themselves as a new creation. They struggle to see their full potential in God. No matter what people say, they cannot receive an identity that goes beyond their struggles. Spiritual slavery will even sabotage any loving empowerment or breakthrough God sends their way.

Unfortunately, the slave mentality also impacts how they see other people. Quite often we view others not in how they actually are, but in how we see ourselves. That is why Jesus taught us to be careful in picking out a speck in someone's eye while ignoring the plank in our own. Slaves, over time, become judgmental and critical of the world and have become blinded to the areas in their own life that need change. They have not been able to receive the love and grace of God, so they struggle to give that out to the world.

7. SLAVES LOOK OUT FOR THEMSELVES.

The driving force in spiritual slavery is survival, so you enter situations thinking, *"How does this affect me?"* There is not as much thought about *"how does this affect those around me?"* There is little focus about others in the family, only how life and circumstances affect *"number one."*

When spiritual slaves become leaders, they are more concerned with entitlement than humbly blessing and serving people. They can also have an eye on bottom line results more than relational health and genuine connection. Honor fills the hearts of sons, while slaves have no problem manifesting betrayal, dishonor and cynicism.

Slaves don't empower other people, they look to empower themselves; rather than celebrating the people around them. Sadly, with a spiritual slave, there is little inheritance passed down. The legacy ends when their work ends.

Meanwhile sons eventually become fathers, raising up a new generation of empowered spiritual sons and daughters who can carry the inheritance to the next level.

THE POWER OF FATHERING

The only way that spiritual slavery will be broken over

the body of Christ is when true spiritual fathers rise up to mentor sons and daughters of the generation. But it's important to know that a slave cannot become a spiritual father. Only sons can eventually become fathers.

That is why the first step to changing this spiritual bondage of slavery is for us all to learn how to be sons and daughters. We must learn to let Father God teach us how to be sons before Him and how to be brothers and sisters to each other. Once sons walk their process out, an organic transition takes place where they begin to father others, though never leaving the foundation of sonship.

This transition will help bring about what Malachi prophesied about for the last days. The key to the massive transformation that is needed involves the healing of fathers and sons, mothers and daughters.

Behold, I will send you Elijah the prophet before the coming of the great and dreadful day of the Lord. And he will turn the hearts of the fathers to the children, and the hearts of the children to their fathers . . . Malachi 4:5-6

APPLYING THE PROCLAMATION OF FREEDOM

In 1863, Abraham Lincoln made one of his most famous speeches as the sixteenth president of the United States. During the Civil War, soldiers were enmeshed in a turbulent fight against neighboring states. Throughout this struggle, President Lincoln sought not only to bring peace, but also worked vigorously to end the demeaning practice of slavery in the United States.

Titled the *Emancipation Proclamation*, Lincoln gave an executive order as Commander in Chief that proclaimed the freedom of slaves, initiating a major shift in our nation's values and practices regarding a race of people that had previously been devalued and dishonored.

The proclamation itself did not end slavery, but set into motion a nationwide effort to stop the practice and further laws that brought ex-slaves into recognition as citizens of the United States. Even though Lincoln's speech was stirring, there was subsequently much work to be done. Not only did a Constitutional amendment need to be passed, requiring grueling effort, decades of laws and renewal needed to take place to make that declaration a reality.

Slaves not only needed to be recognized as citizens, they needed to know how to live outside of slavery. A cultural transformation was needed to make room for the change.

You and I have a promise of sonship that is available for us to grasp right now. We have a privilege of living as sons, accepted before our Father in heaven and empowered with the Spirit His Son carried. It is one thing to renounce spiritual slavery in your life. It is an entirely new thing to learn and practice the ways of sonship.

QUESTIONS FOR CONSIDERATION:

1. Where are you recognizing that you think like a spiritual slave instead of a son?
2. Which characteristics of spiritual slavery stuck out the most to you?
3. What makes it difficult to move out of a slave mindset and into sonship?
4. What would change in your life if you made the shift from slavery to sonship?

PRAYER

Father God, I acknowledge the areas in my life where I have served the mindset of a slave. I recognize that You have not called me to be a slave, but a son. I take responsibility today for agreeing with "slavery thinking" and I want to be free from it. I declare today that I will no longer serve You God according to a slave mentality, but I will take my freedom as a son (or daughter) once and for all. I repent for living with and agreeing with slave thinking.

I renounce where I came into agreement with slavery. I renounce living as an orphan, for living as a pauper, for giving into a distorted lens, for having little vision and for lacking an identity. I renounce covering up my insecurities and living out of fear. I renounce living out of self-reliance and not letting anyone speak into my life, for not handling hard times like a son, but as a victim to my circumstances.

I am not a slave. I am a son! I choose to take my place as a son and to embrace the love that God has for me as my Father. I am accepted by Him and I embrace that today. In Jesus' name. Amen.

THE TRAP OF PERFORMANCE-BASED LIVING

Much of our world loves to push the limits in order to attain great results. Yet in the yearning for achievement, we have fallen in love with performance-based living. Millions of people give their life over to accomplishment and constant busyness in order to gain a sense of fulfillment. Yet they never seem truly satisfied.

And at what cost are we doing this?

Our world is packed with unfulfilled performers, seeking for love and validation in what they do. Unfortunately, the virus of performance has been invading Christianity since its birth. The Apostle Paul confronted the Galatian church by asking, *"Did you receive the Spirit by the works of the law, or by the hearing of faith?"* (Galatians 3:2) Law-based living continues to this day under the guise of performance-based Christianity.

When performance invades Christianity, well-meaning believers seek to gain a sense of love from God by doing things for Him and following religious duties. This is all done to make ourselves feel spiritually and emotionally validated.

Yet at its core, performance negates the power of the cross and what Jesus paid for. What was given freely is exchanged for religious striving, perfectionism and achievement. Giving ourselves to the work of God is a loving offering to Him, but the motive that drives a lot of what we call "Christian service" is driven by performance.

Performance based Christianity negates the power of grace and God's unconditional love for His children. We end up carrying an unnecessary burden that God has actually freed us from. Yet if we don't have the love of God and His approval implanted in our hearts, performance is an easy temptation.

SIGNS OF PERFORMANCE BASED CHRISTIANITY

Church life all around the world display the signs of performance-based Christianity. You can see it in the following mindsets people carry. Performance based Christianity says, "I feel loved and fulfilled based on:"

- *How much and how often I read the Bible.*
- *How regular and intense my prayer life is.*
- *How much of the Bible I know, can quote and how many theological arguments I can win.*
- *How holy I seem to be living my life.*

- *How often I attend church and maintain involvement.*
- *How many results I am producing.*
- *What spiritual routines and acts of service I have under my belt.*
- *How much service I give to God or how long I have been a Christian.*

DEFINING PERFORMANCE BASED LIVING

With a "performance lifestyle," *your value, worth and identity are based on what you do and how well you do it.* Your sense of well-being hinges on your daily labors. The word "performance" is not an evil word, but it was never meant to define your identity.

It's all about what is motivating you on the inside. There can be two athletes playing the field; one is motivated by performance pressure and the other is not. Two singers can present on the stage; one being driven by performance and the other not. "Performance living" cannot be identified simply by observing behavior, but by recognizing unhealthy motives in the heart.

THE LIES OF PERFORMANCE

The greatest way you can identify performance is when you live under pressure. A series of lies come along that keep the pressure of performance intact.

- *I must excel or achieve to belong or be accepted.*
- *My performance gives me status in life.*
- *I'm secure only when I am productive.*
- *If I do something wrong, it means I am bad.*
- *If I don't perform well, I won't be loved and won't belong.*

WHEN PERFORMANCE BEGINS

Those who carry the performance yoke start off early in life. Most did not receive approval from their parents apart from their achievements. The problem for many is that they actually performed well, so the dysfunctional way of receiving attention and validation was fed.

Of course, there is nothing wrong with receiving affirmation for our accomplishments. But it was never meant to be our core source. We were designed to be loved unconditionally, simply for who we are.

IGNORING THE ISSUES OF THE HEART

So many desire to be healthy and live whole lives, but they also do not want to let go of performance-based living. The pressure of life pulls on the emptiness in their hearts to stay in the cycle.

Even when danger signals arise, like breakdown in the physical body and personal relationships erode, we fail to stop and make adjustments. We are way too addicted to achievement, the drive for success and feelings of accomplishment. Most don't stop unless there is a massive breakdown or it's too late.

SLOWING DOWN TO FACE OURSELVES

Some may try to heal their brokenness by getting a quick book or program, so they can just go back to the same living. They don't realize that breaking free requires a lifestyle change. Nurturing the issues of the heart and dealing with the pain involved not only takes time, but a different pace of living. Performers are so busy there is no time to deal with weakness or brokenness.

Issues of the heart cannot be addressed in a microwave. They must simmer in a crock-pot, allowing for patient processing. The performance trap has taught us to pursue quick fixes; to embrace self-help that promise quick cures and fast results. Yet it only keeps us in the destructive cycle.

I run across this all the time with people who drive for bottom line results, yet sacrifice it on the altar of true relationship. Many people's lives appear amazing with personas that present success. Yet behind the scenes there is a lack of heart health, relational connectivity and true authenticity.

Ask them how work or their latest purchases are and they can give an impressive pitch. But when asked about how their heart is doing, there's very little to discuss. Performance has turned people into machines focused on results and shallow appearances.

A HIGHER VALUE FOR CONNECTION

In Luke 10, Jesus highlighted the performance trap at an occasion where he was invited over Martha's house. This informal gathering would reveal a relational pattern we all need to confront.

Sitting down to connect, Mary engaged Jesus fully, while Martha went into "go mode." *Get busy, get the food ready, serve, do, do, do. We've got to have some food! Someone has to put the meal together!*

Certainly, food has to be prepared. Guests need to be served. The action is not wrong, Jesus was simply confronting a false motive we can all get lost in. For Martha, performance had become something to bury herself in, while her sister Mary learned to make relationship connection the higher priority.

Jesus is not promoting sitting around and waiting for food to drop out of thin air. He is addressing an overriding motive within us that can make doing, serving and performing more important than simple relational connection.

VALUE FOR RELATIONSHIP

Growing up I heard sermons on this text, where the point unanimously made was that we need to spend more time with Jesus and make sitting in His presence a high priority. Although this is a valid point, the church missed an even greater precept. I have watched many Christians run into the prayer closet to spend time with God, yet they have no idea how to authentically connect to other people. Their solitude becomes dysfunctional isolation.

Jesus is not just emphasizing quality time with Himself. The value here is that relational connection is always the higher priority than serving. The gold nugget is that a loving relationship is the greatest place of value in the Kingdom; more than any activity or performance.... period.

A key exercise in breaking out of the performance trap involves making relationships a top priority. We must make non-negotiable time for intimate connection with God, but this must be reflected by our increasing value for loving others and growing in relationships with those around us. Performance strongholds make no time for this, because relationships take them away from the hamster wheel of productivity. Unfortunately, people do not make changes until their performance-based life starts to drastically erode.

MAKING THE COURAGEOUS TRANSITION

I have thoroughly had to address this issue in my own life. Personally, I can attest to the fact that the performance trap will eat up anyone who will listen; chewing them up and spitting them out as a worn-out mess.

During a major spiritual renovation in my life, I confronted the performance trap head on. Like Martha, performance took precedence more often than it should have. My sanity was wearing out quickly, so I knew I needed to make a major overhaul in my life. Performance had become my way of living *every single day* and that had to change.

In order to make the change, I had to renounce living around performance. Although challenging at first, it has been one of the most freeing experiences of my life. Taking the pressure off by resting in the love of God for me was incredibly freeing. I had to take refuge in the fact that I am a son of a Father who loves me and is proud of me. The burden of how people respond is not up to me. I had to release myself to be myself and let the results fall where they may.

REBUILDING THE FOUNDATION

Serving God without experiencing the Father's approval will no doubt open a door to a performance lifestyle. Rejection's desire is to keep you performing to earn your sense of acceptance and validation. God has an identity for you, but it is not based on your performance. He designed you to live *from* who you already are in Him. Getting free will take honest recognition, courageous changes and a daily lifestyle transformation.

A major connection in breaking free from performance is learning to understand, *My identity is not based on what I do. It's based on the fact that I am a loved child of God.* We are human *beings* not human doers, so the transition needs to be made on how we feel loved and valued.

God designed each of us to enjoy Him and each other in relationship. Breaking free of performance-based living will involve seeing the value in simple connection.

From SJ Hill's Book "Enjoying God":...*you weren't made to find your identity in the stuff you do. You were made to be in relationship with God. The Father doesn't define your life by what you do. He defines your life by who He created you to be for Himself. He doesn't want your efforts as much as He wants you. He enjoys your worship. He enjoys your dance. He enjoys the times that you think about Him. But most of all, He enjoys you.*[2]

AN INTENTIONAL CHANGE

For many of you, there are not many references for how to do this, so it will take some daily reflection and heart change. There is an image that God sees you to become in your identity, and you cannot move towards it through performance. Transformation will not manifest by doing more or finding another avenue to perform. Your motives will need to be honestly addressed. Time will need to be given towards a pace based on yielding to God, not striving to attain His love.

---

[2] S.J. Hill, Enjoying God: Experiencing Intimacy with the Heavenly Father (Relevant Books, 2001)

138

We will also have to confront the lie that if we are not driven in performance, we will not excel in life. We have to admit that although performance brings an initial high, it will, in the long term, steal peace, joy and health.

DETOXING PERFORMANCE LIVING

We are going to have to let go of the false affirmation we feel when we perform well. This does not mean that we reject affirmation or stop the enjoyable things we do. We simply allow God to shift the motivation. We change our core source of affirmation to how God feels about us. We learn to live days in contentment of just being God's kid. We stop living for approval and we live *from* approval. With God as your Father, you already have His love.

People who are chronic performers often experience initial withdrawal symptoms as they begin moving away from performance living. Recognize that some days you will squirm and not know what to do with yourself. Be at peace, because that is a sign you are in transition. Give yourself time to make the shift.

For those of you who base your identity on your work, you may need to take a vacation, sabbatical or leave of absence to get away and reset your heart. You will need to go through the awkward pain of not having work as your core validation. Then begin to reset your identity based on God's love for you and who He created you to be, simply as His child.

THE PRESSURE IS OFF

I have a personal routine that I practice whenever I am speaking or am called into help a difficult situation.

Performance pressure may want to enter whenever I am involved in these kinds of situations. I say the following prayer to remind myself of who I am and where my love comes from.

Father I am Your son. You love me already and You are proud of me. I have nothing to prove today. I owe these people nothing but to love them. And at the same time, You love them more than I could ever love them. So, I am just going to be myself and let You work through me in anyway way You desire. I am confident in that. I plan to have fun all throughout, because the pressure is off!

The funny thing is, when performance pressure is removed, our "performance" can actually improve drastically. Why? Because when there is no pressure, stress is alleviated, and energy can be used for enjoyment and effectiveness.

QUESTIONS FOR CONSIDERATION:

1. In what ways has your identity been wrapped up in what you do? How do you find performance-based living working in your life? When did it begin?
2. In what ways does performance infect your relationship with God?
3. Where do you find yourself still performing for people's approval?
4. Where has performance led you into mindsets like perfectionism and people pleasing?
5. In what areas is God calling you to break out of performance-based living?
6. How can you move to a place where you are living more simply as God's child? What does that look like?

PRAYER

Father God, I acknowledge where I have served the performance mindset in areas of my life. I recognize that You have not called me to be a slave, but a son. I take responsibility today for agreeing with the performance mindset and I want to be free from it. I declare today that I will no longer serve God according to a slave mentality, but I will take my freedom as a son (or daughter) once and for all.

I acknowledge that Jesus did not die on the cross so I could be bound with performance burdens and works based pressure. I fully accept the grace and unconditional love of God today in my life.

I repent for living with and agreeing with performance thinking. I renounce where I came into agreement with a performance mindset and way of living. I renounce living as though I needed to perform to earn Your love and other's love.

I let go of mindsets that are tied to performance-based living, like people pleasing, false responsibility, perfectionism and other burdens you have not called me to carry. I release my heart to live in the freedom of Your love and grace.

Today, I am free to be myself, because I am accepted in the beloved. I do not need to earn the love of anyone, including You, Father. I choose to take my place as a son (or daughter) and embrace the love that You have for me as my Father. I am accepted by You and I embrace that today. In Jesus' name. Amen.

WHEN NEED IS ON OVERLOAD

E veryone is born with an inherent need to be noticed and valued for who they are. We long to be encouraged and nurtured into our fullest potential with encouragement and affirmation. When we are noticed and validated in healthy ways, our hearts are filled and our journey becomes empowered.

Experiencing healthy fulfillment in these areas reminds us that we matter. We gain fuel to face challenges and grow to higher levels when we are affirmed in healthy ways. No one has genuinely said, *"I hate being encouraged! Can you please stop!?"* That is because we were designed to be empowered through encouragement, affirmation and validation.

UNMET NEEDS THAT BECOME EXCESSIVE

There is just one problem. Most people don't have a lot of those empowering experiences. Going all the way back to childhood, those deep needs were never met, so we were left empty. To make matters worse, our hearts were crushed with negative experiences, where deep wounds took residence.

What began as legitimate needs are now inflamed with excessive needs that are out of control. What was once a love tank has now become a love tanker, filled with holes that don't allow us to be filled or satisfied.

As a result, rejection drives us to find connection and attention in unhealthy ways. We plunge ourselves into dysfunctional relationships, with the hopes that someone will notice us. Our actions become more focused on meeting our unmet needs than on healthy connection. In fact, excessive neediness keeps us from knowing what healthy connection even looks like. We can become so driven to meet our needs that we lose awareness to how we are coming across.

This is how rejection keeps us bound — by locking us to our neediness so that we are never restored. It keeps us from letting God truly heal those places. So, we demand continual attention and help from others, while draining everyone of energy. Once their resources are exhausted, they throw their hands up, not knowing how to help us anymore. Meanwhile, rejection whispers in your ear, "*See, those people don't love you.*" And we continue to remain stuck in our relationships.

A TICKING TIME BOMB

I know for a fact that if someone carries excessive neediness, at some point they are going to get mad at me.

Some kind of setup will make it seem like I don't love them. The rejection in them is looking to see when someone will reject them like past people did. When they are looking for rejection, they will find it. Remember, rejection likes to be rejected.

You often have to be 100% "on watch" around these people, because anything you say can and will be used against you in a twisted way. People who deal with others that have excessive neediness often walk away saying, *"I can't win."*

Here are some patterns that can manifest from childhood all the way into our adult years, revealing the unmet need to be validated, affirmed and recognized.

THE WALKING RESUME:
"The Need to Feel Important"

I am utterly shocked that I can spend a social hour with a person and never be asked one solitary thing about myself. The entire conversation is immersed in dialogue that points back to the other person. Momentarily realizing they have been talking about themselves way too much, they throw a question out. As I begin to respond, they cannot help themselves but jump right back into where they left off.

They have an excessive *want* for people to validate them.

People who struggle with this often "cast their line," hoping somebody will take the bait and give them the validation they need. Their narrative is littered with an endless description of personal accomplishments, trophies, titles and positions that have been achieved in their life. They rattle off about things they can do, what they know and provide all the stories to prove it.

THE EXCESSIVE TALKER:
"The Need to be Heard"

Everyone has an excessive talker in their life; someone who does not know when to hit the pause button and listen. They don't just talk, they over talk with a turbo shot in it.

One person in particular I remember years ago had this pattern just about every time I talked with him. Gary would talk endlessly. When I would try to insert some truth or contribution to the scenario he was speaking of, he would not acknowledge what I said and continued on with his story.

After running into this continually, I thought, *"How can he be so self-unaware? Doesn't he recognize this pattern? What will it take for him to see how he comes across? Can't he read the body language of people checking out?"* I knew rejection was the root, but I was curious, *"What is the set up in his life that kept him in this incessant pattern of talking?"*

What I learned was that he carried a wound in his heart that said, "not heard." Anytime that "not being heard button" was hit, you would see him talk more and then at times become angry. People were drained and walked away. He eventually claimed that people were unloving and uncaring.

EXCESSIVE ATTENTION SEEKER:
"The Need to be Seen"

Rejection will train us to have a constant urge to be seen and noticed. This occurs in small or large group settings. For those who have a need to be noticed, they will do things in the gatherings that demand everyone's attention. They often take over and dominate conversations.

Those with an excessive attention-seeking pattern often drain an organization of its resources and efforts. A lot of time is often spent giving attention to this particular person. They use any means necessary to gain attention. They might bring up something great about themselves or something difficult they are going through. They will use anything to get the focus drawn on themselves.

Nine times out of ten, this starts when they are very young, often because they never received the proper attention and focus their heart needed. Parents did not attend their sports games or acknowledge their accomplishments, so they live to find applause anywhere they can. It can also work in children who have very loving and attentive parents, but the child carries a rejection mindset that demands an unrealistic level of attention from the family. If this rejection stronghold is not properly dealt with in the child, they will carry it all the way into adult life.

When we live needy, we expect others to love us, especially in the areas where we were unfulfilled in our past. The problem is, that need is never truly filled. This pattern repeats until the bondage is confronted.

THE CONSTANT DOER:
"The Excessive Need to be Valued"

These individuals are always going, going, going….doing, doing, doing, with no sign of resting or stopping. They have connected their self-worth and value with being needed to do something. Their identity is completely wrapped up in what they do for other people. Whether it is caring for someone or helping people in need, they immerse themselves into constant helping and doing without any boundaries or limits. When not doing, they feel empty, lonely and purposeless.

Those who are constant doers are often deep people pleasers. They live their lives carrying the expectations and burdens of others, while often ignoring their own heart and emotional health. They absolutely hate it when someone does not like them or people are unhappy with them. Instead of living intentionally, they live in reaction to everyone else. Rejection keeps them in this toxic lifestyle.

We can immerse ourselves deeply in religious activities; helping everyone we see. The core motivation is still an excessive need to be valued. This does not mean we should stop helping people. The point is that serving others is so much more fruitful and effective when we address the motive behind it. If we don't, we will easily burn out. It is not that helping is wrong, but the improper motivation in your heart that contaminates the good deeds.

THE LITIGATOR KNOW IT ALL:
"The Need to be Right"

When rejection is a part of our thinking, we can develop an unwavering need to be right. The excessive need to be right drives the behavior of a "know it all." They make great debaters, but having relationship with them is a nightmare. Their wounds have cultivated a defensive posture that becomes covered in pride. They cannot step back and quiet the need to fight back. They become the *litigators* in relationships.

This is the husband who gets defensive when his wife is simply trying to help him see something that he is doing that may be hurting the family. It's the boss who can never be wrong. It is the friend who can never say *I'm sorry*. It's the person who *must* make their point, no matter how much you try to reason with them.

Litigators often cut others off quickly in discussions and don't listen. The only thing that matters is their perspective. They can end up cutting off relationships over petty arguments. They are often the bullies we encounter in life.

When we grow in maturity, we value loving a person more than being right. Humility becomes the exchange of healthy living. With love, we win regardless of whether we are right or wrong in the argument. I have personally learned that conflict resolution is more than just winning an argument. The highest level of relationship is one where love can grow and forgiveness can be made available.

THE CODEPENDENT:
"The Excessive Need for Someone Else"

Neediness drives us to look to a person as an emotional source for our well-being. What started as a helpful relationship can move into codependency if one does not deal with the rejection issues of the heart. Codependency is the pattern where we rely upon another person as a source for our sense of identity, love and happiness. We base our well-being on how they are doing and how they act towards us. They become our compass and source rather than God.

When we are not solid in our own identity, we can attach ourselves emotionally to someone as a source for help. This can occur in any relationship dynamic. The addiction here involves another person:

- *A parent regarding their child.*
- *A wife and her husband and vice versa*
- *A dating relationship*
- *A friendship*
- *People in a church, a pastor or leader.*

It takes great courage to recognize codependency in your heart. People can tell you that you are codependent, but you will defend your actions and angrily resist correction. The only way for this to really break is to see in your own heart that this pattern has stolen your ability to walk in wholeness.

The answer to codependency is not independence, for that is another problem in itself. Independence sees no need for the help of others in our life. The answer is *interdependence.* Someone who lives interdependently knows how to receive *and* give out in a healthy way.

MAKING THE SHIFT

How do we begin to make changes and break the dysfunctional patterns that Satan has trained us in? Here are some things we can be mindful of in making adjustments that will breathe life into our relationships.

1. Let the need of your heart be filled with God's love, affirmation and validation. Begin to once and for all acknowledge and receive the love God has for you. John Eldredge stated it so well when he said, *"We are created by God with an infinite capacity to be loved and enjoy love, because we were created to relate to a Heavenly Father who has an infinite capacity to love us!"* When you come to God, you are not interacting with a Father who has an empty tank and little love left to give you. He is overflowing with what your heart needs. Come and pour your heart out to Him.

2. *At some point you will have to stop making people your source for love, affirmation and validation.* We should never isolate ourselves from relationships, but we cannot make people the source for our well-being. We cannot put a demand on people that only God can fill, so release those around you. They cannot be and never will be God.

We all need encouragement and we should never reject it when it comes. However, when we have this never ending, excessive need to get people's approval, it will not have the landing it needs. The toxicity gets further embedded when we seek out what people think of us. Tune your heart to the voice of Father God, who loves you and accepts you right now. His words will give you the steadiness and satisfaction you long for.

3. *Start affirming, validating and loving others.* Do not wait for that day, somewhere over the rainbow, where you will feel completely healed. Start getting out there and become a healing vessel, pointing people to the love of God by loving on them. If you were not given it, then get it from God and give it to others. Don't wait until you feel you have been filled, because in properly letting love out, God will meet you and give you more.

4. *Learn to love, affirm and validate yourself.* Quite often, we can find ourselves in situations where there is no one around to affirm us and give us the validation that our heart desires. This is where we often have to learn to love ourselves and speak words of kindness that validate, affirm and express the acceptance our heart longs for. David learned to encourage himself in the Lord, and we as believers need to learn to affirm ourselves, too. With our words, we can begin to fill the emptiness in our heart that is longing for wholeness.

QUESTIONS FOR CONSIDERATION:

1. In what relationships can you find yourself being excessively needy or demanding?
2. What are the unmet needs in your heart that you seek to find in others in a way that is not healthy?
3. Of the patterns mentioned in this chapter, which one(s) do you see in your life that need to be addressed? Define what it looks like to grow out of those areas. Take some time to talk it out with someone and write it down.
4. Take a moment to ask God to heal that place in your heart that is needy.
5. Where do you need to begin the practice of speaking words that validate, affirm and express the acceptance your heart longs for?
6. Make an action plan. What are some actions you can take to affirm that God loves you and break these patterns of neediness?

PRAYER:

I ask You, Father, in the name of Jesus Christ that You would help me learn to recognize my neediness. I ask that You help me to no longer operate from the position of desperate neediness. Your love satisfies, so I come to You to be filled with Your affirmation and validation. I release those around me from having to meet the needs that only You can fill.

I come out of agreement with excessive and unhealthy neediness for validation, recognition and attention. I repent for these mindsets. I renounce them. Release me from this burden.

Father, fill my heart with Your love, affirmation and validation. I acknowledge Your love and I receive it now. I thank You for it. I come out of agreement with my neediness that keeps me in this pattern.

Forgive me for having a distorted lens regarding You and Your love. Correct my spiritual vision so that I can see and receive from You and others the way you intended me to. I am growing in loving myself and I am growing in being more loving to others. I release the neediness that rises up and I hand it over to You God. In the name of Jesus, release myself, from the programming of neediness that has taken root in me. I will find my peace and satisfaction in You. In Jesus name, amen.

THE COMMUNICATION
TWISTER

With every relationship problem, there is always a communication issue along with it. Twisted communication is responsible for ruining more lives, destroying more churches and ravaging harm in more families at an increasing rate of speed. If we could all improve how well we listen, how we speak to each other and the stories we believe about each other, it would revolutionize how we are able to live as the family of God.

When rejection is in operation, healthy relationships don't have a chance. The end result can be division and disaster. Entire organizations can be completely shattered and collapse as a result of these rejection tactics. This is because rejection twists and distorts communication.

We have all been in those situations where communication gets out of hand. There are those debates that every married couple gets into, where arguing escalates to a point where they don't even remember what they're fighting about. How many times have you been in a conversation where the more you talk the worse it gets?

Ever try to compliment someone by saying, *"That's a nice dress you have on today"* and they reply, *"Why, because I didn't look nice yesterday?"* Ever been locked in an endless cycle of back and forth conversation with someone, where you feel like they have a locked-in perception of you that messes up the interaction? Do you feel absolutely exhausted in achieving healthy conflict resolution with certain people? Odds are that rejection has tainted the lens and has poisoned the potential for healthy interaction to occur.

THE TANGLED WEB

I remember the countless meetings, endless phone conversations and pages of email communication I went through to try and bring resolution to relationship issues. The harder I tried the worse the interactions got. The more I talked, the more my words got twisted and my motivations were questioned.

The communication got scrambled and interpreted in a way I never intended. Without the understanding of spiritual warfare and the enemy's desire to distort communication, I would have constantly remained stuck. I learned the hard way how rejection smudges the lens by which we communicate.

Think of the top five most difficult conversations you have ever had. I know I have my list and they were doozies! Think of someone who just didn't want to arrive at resolution with you. Rejection was at the root system feeding it all.

THE DAMAGING FILTER

The sad truth is that most of the time, we do not hear what is actually being said to us. We are listening through a filter; a personal interpretation of what we hear. Our deep belief system and perspectives give a spin to the communication that comes our way.

If rejection is your filter, then prepare to have a world of chaos in your relational interactions. With this distorted lens, you will always see life and others through a negative, defeated and rejected lens. Before people even open their mouths to speak, you will have a negative perspective about them. The lens is usually filled with, *"He doesn't love me. He doesn't care. He's not even going to listen to what I am saying."* Before a person even talks to you, they are already dead in the water.

Under the influence of rejection, *you will become used to being rejected.* Its ways will become so familiar that you anticipate rejection, attract rejection and find something that validates rejection. Eventually, you'll find yourself backed into a corner, where you see everyone else as the problem.

WARFARE OVER COMMUNICATION

If I am the devil, all I need to do is interfere with your communication. If I can mess with how you hear things and then get you to speak words that stir up the pain a little more, then I can drag you into a roller coaster of dysfunction.

The enemy hates love and seeks to distort and pervert it.

This is because when the love of God fills a person, that love reaches other people and lives are changed. When we become separated from love, we slowly start to collapse inside. The majority of our breakdown in wholeness, and even in health, often comes down to a breakdown in relationships.

Here is what happens when our relationships become twisted by rejection.

- *We assume the worst before a discussion even happens.*
- *Our ability to hear what is really being said is twisted, therefore, what we say back is toxic.*
- *There becomes a distorted sense of self-awareness.*
- *We lose the ability to hear fruitful correction or feedback.*
- *Unhealthy assumptions form that create an inaccurate story about someone.*
- *We blame and accuse others while ignoring personal responsibility.*
- *We minimize our sinful actions while magnifying another's.*
- *Suspicion is mistaken for discernment.*
- *We become very easily offended and hurt.*
- *We find ourselves more and more isolated.*

TOUCHY CONVERSATIONS

Do people have subjects they just cannot bring up in your presence? Do you have those "don't go there" signs on different areas of your life? No matter how perfect the timing or how loving people come across, when someone has touchy nerves of pain, they will not let you go there.

I remember praying with a group of leaders and feeling

a nudge from the Holy Spirit to clear the air with a female member of the group. I shared, *"please forgive me if I have wronged you in any way or come across in any way that was not helpful to you."* I couldn't remember a specific incident, I just felt something was not right between the two of us.

As soon as I shared that, she let out a rolodex of wrongs I had done. It was like she was waiting for the moment to pull them all out. As she blasted me in front of the group, I was overwhelmed and actually wished I didn't bring it up to begin with. I was not interacting with someone who wanted to make our relationship right.

You can tell within a few moments if you are dealing with someone who can be reasoned with. But if rejection is in the midst, there is no chance in the conversation becoming fruitful. Even if the meeting seems to go well, the person can take a twisted translation of what was said away from the discussion.

CANNOT BE REASONED WITH

Those easily offended people become hard to please in any way, because they are looking for something to be offended at. Their broken heart has kept them suspicious in relationships, projecting a battle, even if is not even there. They question the motives of everyone. People are often forced to tiptoe around them, because they have such an intense expectation of people.

Because of deep, unmet needs that exist in the hearts of many, they can demand that others meet their personal expectations. We expect people to know what we need and to love us in the exact way that we need. If the need is not exactly met in the way they want, it triggers anger and hostility.

REJECTING OTHERS BEFORE YOU ARE REJECTED

I often find people saying, "*I don't like that person.*" If you ask them why, they'll say, "*I just don't like them.*" They don't really have a reason, but there is this negative feeling they are running with.

Rejection wants to be rejected, so it will also orchestrate experiences that make it appear as though you are being rejected. We find ways to disqualify someone before we ever get the chance to get to know them. A rejection mindset says, "*You will reject me. So, I will find a reason to reject you before you have the chance to reject me.*"

The key is, we are doing anything we can to stop people from getting close. We judge and quickly write off people as arrogant or self-righteous. We make judgments without ever getting to know the person. It's all to protect ourselves, but we end up pushing great relationships away. People don't have an opportunity to share life with you, because you are not letting them in.

The Bible says whatever we sow into is what we will reap (Galatians 6:7). So, whatever we invest in with our beliefs, our thoughts and our actions will be what we reap in the harvest of our lives. Many people do not realize they are sowing daily into a rejection mindset, which then reaps interactions and experiences that all validate that rejection.

REJECTION PICKS A FIGHT

When people live life looking through the lens of rejection, they are not used to healthy interactions. They cannot truly handle someone loving on them or living in a peaceful relationship, so fights are stirred up easily. If someone loves you more than you love yourself, you will find a way to sabotage that relationship. Picking a fight is usually the most common way.

This initiates a "relationship dodge ball." One person says something from a place of hurt that the other translates with their own hurt and then reacts by hurling back words that intensify the conflict. This keeps the dodge ball flying back and forth.

Marriage is the biggest arena where this problem manifests. Men often enter marriage with rejection issues regarding women, while females enter marriage with strongholds of rejection regarding other males. So, both parties come into the relationship with rejection-tarnished lenses that may bring out defensiveness in the other person. For too many, it is a setup for disaster.

THE REJECTION SETUP

In social settings, people who carry rejection will find themselves getting ignored, forgotten or cast aside. Have you ever noticed that at a party or social gathering you will accidentally ignore or not pay attention to a certain person? If you stop to think about it, there are certain people who we do this with. It is part of the enemy's plan to make a person believe that they are in fact, rejected.

After careful observation, I've found that I, too, have

unknowingly ignored people who carry these kinds of rejection issues. My wife would look at me and say, *"I think you totally ignored that person."* I would respond in shock, thinking, *"I totally did not mean to ignore them in any way."* Then the next time I saw them, the same pattern would occur, even though I consciously tried to pay more attention to them. After a number of situations playing out this way, it dawned on me, *this is a spiritual setup to convince this person that they are rejected!*

THE TWISTED LENS

The most frustrating manifestation of a rejection mindset is how it twists and distorts communication. Being able to communicate is the primary mechanism we have as humans to have relationship with God or others. Satan knows if those communication lines get distorted, then we are all sunk. Rejection works primarily within the realms of communication between people, twisting our words and meaning so love is not exchanged properly.

In the Old Testament, there is a spiritual picture of Satan's work, described as a giant crocodile-like creature named Leviathan (Isaiah 27:1). One of his characteristics is that he is a twisted serpent, showing us what the adversary is seeking to do--twist and distort communication at any turn.

All Satan has to do is get the communication twisted and fights will ensue everywhere, with separation following. What is being heard is not what is actually being said, but rather a twisted version. This twisted interpretation ignites further problems.

The more you try to explain, the worse things get. If we do not deal with the rejection strongholds in our life properly, this twistedness will be a part of all of our relationships. It will exhaust everyone involved and create division left and right.

Healthy relationships always give the benefit to the other person, assuming the best until you are clearly shown otherwise in direct communication. We have all had gaps in relationship communication. If we choose to fill those gaps with distrust, suspicion and strife, then the enemy wins in being able to distort and eventually split relationships.

FILLING IN THE GAP

Rejection will twist conversations, but it will also create a distorted story whenever there is a lapse in communication. For example, if you call someone or text them and don't hear back, rejection will create a negative meaning as to why you haven't heard from them. Lose touch with someone, rejection will create a negative story as to why you haven't seen them.

I've experienced this countless times, where I have gone out of my way to contact someone repeatedly; only to get little to no response. Negative thoughts would flood through me as I processed what might be going on. At times, these thought streams would lead me to very dark and hurtful places. When I actually sat down with the person, most of my projections were inaccurate. There were other things going on in their life that had nothing to do with me. Despite this, rejection was constantly seeking to plunge me into an abyss of negativity regarding other people's motives towards me.

Since learning this aspect of rejection, I am always coaching people to be careful how they interpret gaps in communication. Until you actually have a chance to sit down and hear someone's heart, beware of how rejection will fill the gaps with destructive, bitter and twisted stories.

THE RISE OF STRIFE

The goal of twisted and distorted relationships is to bring in the monster of strife. When strife shows up in any organization, you can expect every kind of sin to manifest. Strife is a contention and competitive striving that poses people against each other. It doesn't matter the reasons. It does not matter who is right and who is wrong. When strife is in the mix, everyone gets affected.

For where envying and strife is, there is confusion and every evil work. James 3:16 (KJV)

With strife, confusion rules the atmosphere. A lot of times, when working on marriage conflict, I advise the husband and wife to come together and repent for strife. I tell them to get together as a family and cast it out of their home. When this happens, a key door that has allowed garbage to come in is closed. The air soon clears so they can talk and work on the other issues that are hindering the marriage.

Do you have confusion in your church? Do you have confusion in your home? Do you have all sorts of evil taking place? I would encourage you to analyze if there is strife in the midst.

A work of strife plays people in constant competition or keeps them bucking up against each other. It opposes unity in every way shape and form. This is why so many organizations and groups have strongholds like competition, lust, offense, fear, manipulation and all kinds of anger swirling around, causing people to feel like they can't even think straight!

CLEARING UP THE COMMUNICATION

So, what are some things we can do to begin to improve our mindset and look at things with a healthier lens?

1. Address your communication filter. We usually have a filter of communication towards others based on how we feel about ourselves. If we have proper love and acceptance of ourselves, this will pour out to others. It's time we stop pointing at others and deal with our own clogged filter.

2. Be more aware of your own motives. This is where we have to ask God to search our hearts and try our motives. We cannot assume the problem is everyone else. True discernment starts when we become more aware of our toxic motives that drive our interactions.

3. Forgive those who have wronged you. We cannot expect to become free of a rejection mindset if we do not freely learn to forgive and release those who have not loved us properly. God's transformational work is not just about your personal healing, but the healing of relationships all around you.

I see this reality playing true in my life more and more each day. As I take off that lens of rejection and remove bitterness from my life, I see things with greater clarity and compassion. My perspective is not so hostile and angry. I start to see things more like God sees them, giving me compassion for people. I am able to chuckle at things I used to cry about.

4. Stop playing spiritual dodge ball. We have to humble ourselves and stop the strife that keeps us arguing, competing and contending against others. As we humble ourselves under the mighty hand of God, we will position ourselves differently before others.

The only way to end this is for someone to stop returning the dodge ball. They've got to get to the point where they say, *"My Dad in heaven loves me, accepts me and validates me. I'm not interested in fighting. I'm going to stop playing relationship dodge ball. I am going to stop rejecting others and coming at them with anger. It's not about winning an argument. It is not about them. It's about me getting healed in Father God."*

5. Take the pressure off of others to be something for you. Often in our brokenness, we place an undue pressure for people around us to be something big for us. We create an idol of them in our hearts, demanding they love us or nurture us in a way that is unrealistic.

Rejection trains us to have unhealthy expectations of others. If they are not met, then anger and rage rises up. I believe many of you reading this need to release someone that you have put tremendous pressure on to be something for your life and healing — an area only God can fill.

6. Become a better listener. Before you start talking, take some time to stop and listen more. As you change your filter, come to relationships with a better listening ear. Be quicker to listen. Don't assume when you meet someone that people are out to get you. As you listen, you will begin to hear more of the hurt and pain of people's lives. You will see that many people are just like you — trying to find their way and often acting out of their unresolved hurt and pain. This does not mean you will be close to everyone, but it means there is no judgment in the way you see them.

7. Start to assume the best. People who have deep hurt often take pride in assuming the worst, thinking if they do so they will preemptively protect themselves from future hurt. This only keeps us in torment. Many would think that assuming the best in situations is a practice of naivety, when in reality, assuming the worst only breeds worry, control and paranoia. Assuming the best keeps our hearts clear of bitter contamination and positions us for healing in all relationships. God's word says that *"love believes all things"* (1 Corinthians 13:7). People in healthy relationships learn to believe the best in those around them.

QUESTIONS FOR CONSIDERATION:

1. How has rejection hindered communication in your relationships? Where do you find yourself arguing, competing, contending against and being defensive with others?
2. Where can you begin to make adjustments with the relationship lens in your life?
3. Where have you experienced relational rejection in your past? Have you transposed that past hurt onto a new relationship?
4. Can you think of a time when you have experienced "twisted communication?" What was the outcome of this

situation?

5. Have you ever played relational "dodge ball" with someone? What was the result?

6. In what situations is God calling you to take responsibility for how you have been coming across to others and contributing to the conflicts in your life?

7. What adjustments can you make in the way you communicate in your relationships so that you do not give rejection room to operate?

PRAYER:

Father God, I need You to come and heal my heart, especially where I have been hurt and wounded by relationships in the past. I recognize that those past hurts will affect my current relationships. I choose to forgive those who have wounded me, mistreated me and acted unloving towards me.

I ask You to help me to grow in how I listen to what others are saying and to become more mindful of how I come across to others. I want to have better relationships with those around me, so that my life can be more fruitful in the power of love. Help me to renew the lens of how I hear and how I perceive others.

I repent for where I transpose my rejection wounds onto people around me, where I become angry at others for where I expect them to "be something for me." I release those around me from having to be a source in my life. Father God, only You can be the core source of life for me. I release those around me to be themselves, even in their brokenness and relational weaknesses.

God, I ask that You help me to lay down the strife in my home, my church and my place of work. I repent for my part in contributing to the chaos and I ask that clarity from heaven come into my heart.

I repent and renounce the work of strife in every form.

I ask that You deliver me from a twisted lens in my relationships. Help me to see with a lens of compassion, instead of defensiveness, offense and hurt. I ask that You help me be quick to listen, slow to speak and slow to being angry. I ask that You fill me with Your grace, so that I may carry a love that breathes healing into relationships around me. In Jesus' name. Amen.

ONLY FOR THE HUMBLE

Want to know a little secret? There is a simple step involved to begin breaking a rejection mindset. But you may not like it. In fact, it will probably challenge you to the core.

Here it is: *your freedom trail is lined with pit stops where you will need to heal the broken lens regarding authority figures.* Otherwise a close friend of rejection will follow you all throughout your life....a subtle destroyer called rebellion. It ways can be more deceptive than you think.

Here is an easy test to see if you struggle with rebellion: *Have someone tell you to do something, especially from an authority figure in your life.*

Yes, it's that simple. Have someone tell you to do something, give you instruction about your life and bring some kind of corrective word. If something inside of you immediately rises up to defend, buck or lash out in anger then you may have rebellion. Most people cannot handle this type of intervention into their life because they have not learned to live as sons before God. They remain in slavery, doing things their own way, by their own standards with no input from authority. If you don't have an authority figure in your life to test this with, then rebellion has probably already begun its work.

UNHEALTHY AUTHORITY REFERENCES

The subject of authority brings up a lot of pain for people. Parents, pastors, leaders and bosses have misused their God-given position in ways that deeply damaged those they were in charge of. Abuse runs rampant and most people do not have healthy references for what a safe leader can be. In fact, I spend a lot of my work helping people unwind themselves from abusive authority figures.

The challenge is that God wants to heal our wounds and instill a healthy perspective towards leadership, regardless of how they treat us. I never advocate for tolerating abuse, but it is critical to keep a heart of honor, despite the toxicity that exists amongst leaders.

Many who come out of unhealthy organizations unknowingly come into agreement with a dishonoring and rebellious lens towards leaders in general. Their pain often gives them a sense of entitlement to be cynical, judgmental and dishonoring. Negative perspectives are cultivated as they begin to separate themselves from any authority figure. Over time, we can lose the blessing of what loving leadership can provide for our destiny.

REBELLION SPAWNED BY REJECTION

Rebellion is deeply tied to the rejection root, because

rejection communicates a narrative that *God and people do not love you. Leaders are not safe.* Rebellion says, *get away from authority figures. You don't need them. Do life on your own.* It grabs a hold of your hurt and convinces you to take life into your own hands.

Now, there are a number of unsafe leaders out there. Trust me, I have met them and have attempted to help many of them. I've even been emotionally abused by a few. But there are also some amazing men and women out there who are doing a tremendous job of making people feel safe in their journey.

THE GOAL OF REBELLION

Rebellion will keep you from healthy relationships with authority. As challenging as it can be, God designed authority figures to often carry the blessing needed for us to go further.

This is why many people often remain stuck in their walk. They have been hurt by authority. Instead of healing from the specific wounds and keeping an honoring heart, rebellion teaches them to run from authority figures.

INDEPENDENCE WITH REBELLIOUS UNDERTONES

People come up to me all the time and share the great exploits they are pursuing. I hear about new ministry ventures, churches and business prospects they have in mind. Yet there is a common thread that is concerning. They are doing this all on their own with no connection to a leadership influence. Some are in this situation because no leadership would help. That is understandable. But many are avoiding the help of leadership input all together.

They start a business with no mentoring. A church gets planted more out of a person's broken need to run something on their own. They say continually, *My ministry, My calling, My thing, I am on My own…*

In nine out of ten of these scenarios, the person is hurt. They are responding to that hurt of not being validated, recognized or cared for. Their perspectives are propelled by unresolved hurt. It's like they have something to prove.

REBELLION AND WITCHCRAFT

The Bible considers the work of rebellion as equal to the work of witchcraft (*For rebellion is as the sin of witchcraft.* 1 Samuel 15:23). Most would think of witchcraft as a sorcerer or someone giving spells or incantations, yet there is so much more to it. The work of witchcraft has a lot to do with control and manipulation.

The common thread in both witchcraft and rebellion is *they both tempt us to take matters into our own hands in toxic ways.* Witchcraft does it through manipulation and control, while rebellion does it by separating from authority. All brokenness can lead us to rebellion and witchcraft, eroding the future health of loving relationships.

In 1 Samuel, King Saul made a decision that went against the clear instruction given by Samuel, Saul's authority figure. Samuel relayed the message from God to completely destroy the possessions of the conquered enemy. Because Saul feared the people, he instead listened to them and kept many of the finer possessions including oxen, sheep and lambs. In his decision, Saul did not heed the Word of the Lord. Instead, his insecurity (rejection roots) made him prey to the demands of the people.

When King Saul disobeyed the direction of authority, we see rebellion was in his heart. Later on, the Bible says that insanity came upon him — a distressing spirit that made him feel crazy (1 Samuel 16:14). Many never make the connection that his breakdown stems from the rebellion that formed in his life.

SEPARATION FROM AUTHORITY FIGURES

Rebellion involves separation from authority figures. Rejection fuels this because it involves relationship separation. When we have not been fathered, we easily become independent and isolated in everything we do.

We don't understand what it means for somebody to have our back. Therefore, rebellion becomes an easy option for many. The problem with a rebellious heart is that we shut ourselves off from favor, blessing and clarity. This is because rebellion lives out a vow that says, *"I am going to do this all on my own."*

THE REJECTION SETUP IN LEADERSHIP

Rejection says to the mind, *See, they don't care. They don't care about you. No one loves you and these leaders doesn't either!* It doesn't matter what the leader does or doesn't do. There is a setup in place to make sure whatever they do comes across as rejection. Rebellion then comes in to give the person a reason to separate from the relationship or to buck any direction that the leader brings to the table.

A classic example of this is in parenting. Rejection can be at work through good parental relationships and bad ones.

A child may perceive that a parent is being unloving, even when the parent may actually be providing a loving correction for the child. Regardless, rejection convinces the child that the parent is being mean or cruel, thus giving them justification to rebel.

KEEPING THE SEPARATION INTACT

Rejection and rebellion hate correction, which is one of the ways that authority figures show us love. It trains people to shut down whenever a leader brings correction or adjustments to our lives.

But rebellion trains us to shut ourselves off from leaders over and over. This leads many to wander from job to job, church to church. Once the relationship gets close and issues come up, the person separates and moves on again. Over time, they live as orphans, going from one orphanage to another.

The only way to freedom is to heal the damaged view of authority. The challenge lies in finding a safe place to work this out. But at the end of the day, it takes forgiveness and the decision to walk with a new slate. Our response to ungodly authority often determines how far we will go in life.

Please understand that no one needs to be a victim. I am not saying that receiving healing and freedom from rebellion should cause us to go back into abusive situations. What I am saying is if we do not heal the wounds that others have caused, we can carry a heart of dishonor and rebellion towards any future authority figures we encounter.

THE DANGER OF ISOLATION

The greatest danger of rebellion is how it will keep you away from fruitful connection. Remember, man was never meant to be alone. Rebellion drives you away from people into what seems like a safe oasis, but it is actually an empty wilderness. It's like being pushed out into the arctic on a floating glacier that slowly melts. You feel free and liberated at first, but slowly you lose your stability. When you cry out for help, you realize there is no one there to rescue you. Not because they are not willing to, but because you have distanced yourself over the years into a place of isolation. You now realize you are alone and deeply struggling with day to day clarity.

Ultimately, God wants to lead you into healthy relationships, whereas Satan constantly pulls you away in rejection, fear and unhealed pain. When we're in rebellion, the temptation to isolate can be intense.

THE SPAWNING OF MENTAL ILLNESS

Let me be upfront with you. Being relationally isolated will mess with your mental sanity over the long haul. In fact, much of our modern day mental illness is further increased because of the breaches in relationship with authority. The hurt is so bad, the pain runs so deep and the walls of separation are thick.

I've spent a lot of my years working alongside people who are battling mental health issues of some form. Be it anxiety, schizophrenia, panic attacks or PTSD issues, I have observed first-hand what abuse from authority figures has caused. And I have also noticed what the unresolved separation from authority figures has done to keep the torment intact.

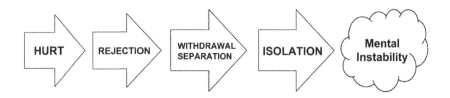

The danger of rebellion is that we become the sole authority on every issue of our life. We lose a sense of checks and balances that help our mental clarity and wisdom. We lose the benefits of sound council, proper mentoring and the ability to be taught. When there are no healthy people around to bring correction or warning, we set ourselves up for a life that lacks sanity.

Way too many believers lack someone in their life that can say, *"I think you are a little off on this."* This is why cultures are flooded with unfruitful decisions and distorted perspectives that keep people in toxic patterns for decades.

BENDING THE KNEE

This was a massive change I had to make in my own life. I had developed some very unhealthy patterns of thinking and behaving in my life. I had Scriptural justification and a whole story behind how I did relationships. The problem was I was way off in a few areas and they were beginning to take a toll on my wholeness.

It wasn't until I humbled myself to some people who could bring me in check that change began to happen in my life. This involved humbling myself before some authority figures, pastors and seasoned people. I had to be able to handle healthy correction as a fruitful experience in my life.

But this isn't easy. Humbling yourself can be one of the most difficult things in the world to do. I had to admit that I wasn't hearing from God as clearly as I was declaring. I had to face the fear that although my way of living was comfortable, it was leading me into more dysfunction and error.

Humbling ourselves before God allows Him to deal with anything and everything. *It's all on the table.* It also opens us up to people who can help point out in love, those areas that need tweaking. A rebellious spirit does not allow us to be corrected, and as a result, we never change and continue to live in bondage.

I had to be willing to hear correction and not fight back. I had to learn to honor those I dishonored in the past. It was very important that I not live to be right, but to walk humbly before my God. Sometimes we need to resist the enemy, but other times, our greatest breakthrough comes when we humble ourselves before God and those He has placed in our lives as authority figures.

QUESTIONS FOR CONSIDERATION:

1. Where has there been a hurt from an authority figure in your life? What was your response?
2. Where has pride had an influence in your spiritual walk? What would true humility look like in that situation?
3. Where has rebellion crept into your life regarding authority?
4. Where do you see dishonor taking place in families, the church and in business?

5. Is there an authority figure that you need to humble yourself with?
6. What action step do you need to take today so that you humble yourself under God's hand?

PRAYER:

Father God, I ask that You help me see where rejection has trained me in rebellion, stubbornness and pride. I ask that you help me to see where I have been deceived, so that I may humble myself and receive the truth.

I recognize where I have at times isolated myself from relationship and blocked off people in my life with a rebellious heart. I also recognize where I have been stubborn or rebellious with authority. I ask that You forgive me for having a wrong heart towards my parents, leaders and overseers.

I repent and renounce the ways of rebellion, which have put a distance between me and people I could be in relationship with. I also see where pride can keep me from receiving the full healing and transformation You have for me.

I don't want to be stubborn anymore. I don't want to isolate myself apart from people You want me to be in relationship with. I realize that I cannot grow in God only by myself. I must connect to the body of Christ and allow myself to grow in relationship with brothers and sisters.

I ask that You heal my heart as I humble myself before You and before others.

I renounce stubbornness as a relational tool. I put away rebellion and I allow my guard to come down, destroying that work of pride in my life. I ask that You show me where these strongholds have come in so that I may walk free in Your power. Thank You for loving me and being patient with me in this process. In Jesus' name. Amen.

16

BREAKING OUT OF PRISON

G od is building in His people an ability to live as overcomers; those who are presented with impossible odds, yet still experience personal breakthrough. We love reading books and watching movies about people who had incredible disadvantages but overcame with relentlessness.

Every single one of us faces a resistance, assigned to wear us down and take us out. We are in the midst of a spiritual war, designed to overthrow the warrior in us and steal our destiny to overcome. Rejection wants to keep us stuck in never breaking free.

Life is tough. No one gets a clean pass in life; this includes Christians. Yet somehow, we can tend to think that following Jesus should make us immune to pain and struggle. Every person has to face their own set of obstacles that can potentially suck the life out of them. At the same time, those areas of challenge can become powerful incubators for our greatest growth.

STEALING YOUR POWER

The resistance that comes against you will seek to keep you living as a victim, rather than an overcomer. It will lead you to a place where you manifest one or more of the following thoughts:

- *I am powerless.*
- *My situation is hopeless.*
- *I have no options.*
- *I have no choices.*

Unfortunately, heart break and woundedness is a part of life. Everyone has experiences where someone should have loved you but did not. It may have even been abusive situations. I've personally worked with people whose list of significant traumas are too many to even count.

Maybe someone observed that were you in pain or experiencing abuse but did nothing to help. It may have been a father who never spoke love and left you in your pain. Maybe it was a family that always ignored you and left you alone in your thoughts all the time.

In moments of trauma and drama, we can become wounded under the power of someone else, leaving us to believe that we are powerless. Many people are passive when it comes to responding to our pain. They often don't know what to do, so they do nothing. This can program us to believe that we are helpless. Not only are we left with damage in our hearts, we also have to reckon with a victim mindset that wants to follow us in life.

The victim mindset takes the negative experiences of our life and projects them onto our future. Therefore, we see the rest of our lives not as victorious, but as prisoners. Negative perceptions start to dominate our thinking. Life just happens to us and we lose the will to overcome.

KEEPING US IN PRISON

Most of us were not given tools to process the healing of our pain, so it can be very easy for our past to define our present and future. Our wounded history can become our identity. Pain and limitations can surround us like a cloud, holding our heart prisoner to the damage we experienced.

If you feel stuck in your pain, this is one of the signs that a victim mindset may be forming. It will not allow you to receive healing from Father God, while keeping you glued to your past heartache. It leaves no room for hope and faith for a new life, free from the disappointments of the past.

SIGNS OF A VICTIM MINDSET

The victim mindset is fueled by rejection. In fact, a victim mindset is rejection's foot soldier to keep you from seeing any picture of potential freedom for yourself. It may work in one area of your life or multiple areas. Here are some signs of its work:

- *There is a driving force to be validated in your pain, so you feel the need to constantly replay the painful stories of the past.*
- *When you meet new people, you feel compelled to make sure they understand your painful story.*
- *You have this constant belief that you always get the short end of the stick in life.*
- *You seem to attract people who abuse you, neglect you, take*

advantage of you, use you, ignore you, etc.

- *You have friends around you that do not challenge you, but allow you to remain in your bondage.*
- *You tolerate abuse in your life from people around you.*
- *You have no idea how to stick up for yourself in a healthy way.*
- *You struggle to have a voice or a clear opinion.*
- *You struggle in even knowing what you want or making that firm decision for change.*
- *You point to your circumstances as the reason for your problems.*
- *You struggle with the courage to fight for what you want.*
- *You often don't even know what you really want.*

STEALING YOUR POWER

The victim mindset comes to steal your ability to stand up, make choices and change. It prevents you from seeing the options you have and ways you can get out of bondage. The bottom line is that it seeks to keep you feeling powerless.

The victim mindset is full of lies, but it throws a few "facts" of your wounded past as evidence that things cannot change. It will highlight negative experiences, even blaming God for not rescuing you. The biggest problem with victim thinking is that it will train you to have a dysfunctional relationship with God, where you wait for something to fall from the sky, rather than taking action because the Holy Spirit lives within you.

A victim mindset will create a narrative on what God is not doing, while keeping you from seeing the powerful work of what He is doing. It's the enemy's way of keeping you from noticing any improvements. There is no room for celebration. No place for acknowledging growth. The narrative is constantly disempowering.

It plays a recording in repeat mode, constantly pointing to circumstantial change as THE only answer. *"If only I had different parents. If only I had a better job. If I could only get some better friends. If I only had a mentor. If only I had more resources. If only..."*

STEALING YOUR VALUE

Victim thinking will make you feel that being rejected and wounded is normal, causing you to believe you don't have worth. It sucks the value right out of you and keeps you stuck, looking for someone to blame as to why you are where you are. It keeps you feeling unworthy and devalued.

A victim mindset will teach you to anticipate the possibility of being hurt by others — projecting it into every relational situation. It can actually train you to feel justified when things go wrong. *"See, I told you. Nothing goes my way."*

MAGNIFIED NEEDINESS

Many who struggle with a victim mindset will seize opportunities to gain attention and bring a focus to their problems and pain. They can end up dominating conversations and doing anything possible to keep attention on themselves. When prayer requests are taken, they monopolize the time with their issues. They drain ministry phone lines with the constant retelling of all that is going wrong.

Neediness becomes a real driving force for them. They

speak excessively about their problems and negativity. If people around are not careful, their desire to help will be abused.

With a victim mindset, you cannot receive from God, because you become too focused on your pain. You will struggle to receive from God, because you will be tempted to think He either caused the pain, or He bailed out on you when you needed Him the most.

JESUS CONFRONTS THE VICTIM MINDSET

Jesus found a sick man by a pool, where many others lay sick and diseased. The location was Bethesda, a supernatural site where an angel would come down and stir up the waters. When the angel touched the waters, the first person to jump in was healed of whatever disease they had. Talk about an amazing opportunity for instant healing!

In this setting, Jesus approached a man who had been afflicted with an infirmity for thirty-eight years. John writes, *"When Jesus saw him lying there, and knew that he already had been in that condition a long time, He said to him, 'Do you want to be made well?"'* (John 5:6).

Jesus knew that this man did not get sick a week ago. This disease had gripped him for most of his life. One thing Jesus knew is that someone who has a disease for a long time can end up wrapping their identity around their infirmity. What comes against us can end up becoming who we are if we are not discerning.

CONFRONTING THE STORY

The question Jesus asks confronts the victim mindset

right from the start. When you read this account, it seems as though Jesus is being a little uncaring, at least by our modern-day standards. He doesn't ask for the man's story. No intake done at all regarding what factors got him to this place. Jesus asks a direct question, *"Do you want to be made well?"* He cuts right to the heart of the matter, *"Do you really want to be healed?*

To the average reader, this seems like a silly question. Who would want to stay sick? As a reader, I am answering the question for the man before he can even speak, *"Yes! Yes! Just say yes!"* We don't read that, but instead, the telling of a story. *"The sick man answered Him, 'Sir, I have no man to put me into the pool when the water is stirred up; but while I am coming, another steps down before me'"* (John 5:7).

Jesus didn't ask that. He just needed a *yes* or *no* answer. A victim mindset doesn't know how to answer that direct question, because it would draw a line of decision in the sand. It would set a new requirement for personal ownership. If he says *yes*, then he is personally responsible from now on. If he says *no*, he looks like a fool to everyone. So instead, he gives a list of reasons why he hasn't been able to get into the pool.

Let's be honest, if he really wanted to be healed, he could pay or even bribe someone. *"Hey buddy, next time the angel comes, I'll give you a thousand dollars if you run and shove me into those waters. Give it all you got and I'll pay you back when I get back on my feet. I'll get a job and earn plenty of money to make it worth your while. Anything....anything to just get in that water. If I don't make it this month, then help me next time. Whatever it takes. Get me in that water!"*

Instead, he was so bound that his answer was ...*the story.*

All of us, if not careful, can carry *a story* within us that is not the story God has given; a narrative littered with chapters of unhealed pain, distorted perspectives and limited thinking. We can carry that story into many different situations, projecting it onto future encounters. The man had a chance to confront his story and replace it with a new one — a story of God's healing power. It is the same story God is bringing to us today, but we have to ask ourselves the same question. *Do I really want to be well?*

CHANGING YOUR STORY

Your painful history never has to be your future. But in order for this to manifest, you will need to let go of the disempowering story you keep replaying that keeps you stuck.

This means we have to let go of retelling all the reasons why we cannot grow, change or break free. A new narrative needs to be embraced, one that provides hope and a future filled with possibilities.

Yet this can only be done when you take personal responsibility for your freedom. It doesn't mean that everything in life is your fault. Don't get into the blame game, as that does nothing to help. Victorious people have a new mindset that says, *"no one can want change for me more than I do."*

WHAT DO YOU WANT?

I have worked with countless people who have been

victimized in some manner. Through physical, sexual, verbal or emotional abuse, they have been damaged to the core and broken of their stability. Harsh experiences like this often strip people of their ability to choose. They lose the power of their voice. They are left as victims.

In the rebuilding process, one of the things I ask is, *"what do you want?"* Many have never even been asked this question before. They've spent their lives bound to their wounded past or a dominating person's influence. My goal is to help them regain their personal power to make decisions and reclaim their voice to say "yes" or "no."

The recovery of who you are is necessary to break the victim mindset. Part of this involves leaving the identity of a victim. A victim needs someone else to rescue them, whereas overcomers recognize the Rescuer that lives in them and they make decisions to walk free.

BREAKING AGREEMENT

Breaking agreement with a victim mindset involves the power of repentance. It's a God-given gift to loosen the chains that bind. I invite people to practice this out loud. Take your voice back. Break agreements with victim thinking and declare your new mindsets.

I cannot do this for you and God will not move your mouth for you. In personal sessions, I often have people stand up to make their declarations. I will even put a sword that I have in my office in their hands. The physical posture leads them to speak with greater authority and conviction.

The power of your mouth needs to be taken back, so that you can speak words which welcome life and hope. Self-pity taught us to use our mouth to complain or project doom and gloom. God teaches us to use our mouth to speak life about those things which redeem and bring possibilities into every circumstance.

EMBRACING GRATITUDE AND THANKSGIVING

A victim mindset can be eradicated by a heart that is grateful. Thanksgiving is the gate into a more empowered perspective. I find it to be one of the most underutilized habits in people's lives, so no wonder so many are trapped in the clutches of limitation.

A victim mindset is covered with ingratitude and complaining. But it is so much more fruitful to walk through adversity with a grateful heart. I have told people for years; *a grateful heart can never be defeated…ever!* With gratitude, you win no matter what happens around you!

TAKE ACTION TO CULTIVATE A NEW LIFESTYLE

Every day we focus on something. Breaking free from the limitations of victim thinking will involve changing what you focus on. As an overcomer, you will need to focus on what you *can* change. One thing I know I can always change is my attitude. If your focus is on what is going wrong or what people did to you, then your focus needs to shift.

This does not mean we ignore our pain. It means we don't wear our pain as our favorite coat. Paul said it best, *"We are troubled on every side, yet not distressed; we are perplexed, but not in despair; persecuted, but not forsaken; cast down, but not destroyed"* (2 Corinthians 4:8-9 KJV).

I love his expression. He didn't deny the problems, like

so many Christians do. He was well aware of the obstacles in his life. He faced them head on, but with a heart that allowed the healing power of God to take what the enemy would use against him for evil, to a place of empowerment and strength.

QUESTIONS FOR CONSIDERATION

1. Where in life have you experienced some difficult and even traumatic experiences that made it hard to move forward?
2. What are some of the impossibilities you face in life? What would happen if you looked at them as an overcomer?
3. In what ways do you fall into victim thinking regarding your life?
4. What action plan can you apply today so that you can take back your life from the clutches of victim thinking?

PRAYER

Father God, I recognize where the victim mindset has become a way of thinking in my life. The battles I have faced and the brokenness I struggle with are wanting to become prisons around me, keeping me from seeing the hope You have for my life. I do not want to be chained to limitations or difficulties any longer.

Today, I do what no one else can do for me: I take responsibility for my freedom. I take my place as a child of God today to stand for my healing and freedom.

I repent and I renounce of victim thinking. I repent and I renounce of taking on a victim mindset. I command the works of those mindsets to be gone in the name of Jesus.

Today I give thanks for who God is. I declare that He is a good God. He is a good Father. I declare today that I am a child who is loved by God. I have what it takes in Christ Jesus to overcome the chains that bind me. I declare today that I will no longer be a victim.

I am not a victim!

I will no longer use self-loathing, self-pity or hopelessness as a way of coping with my problems. I refuse to "check-out" in life and miss out on the victories I can participate in. I command all works of oppression, heaviness and discouragement that keep victim thinking intact to leave in Jesus name. I declare that I am taking my life back as an overcomer! In Jesus' name. Amen.

TAKING BACK YOUR FREEDOM

Experiencing transformation is always a process, but we also need tools to help us break free. This is a journey, and you need action steps to process who God made you to be, while shedding the layers of what rejection has trained you in. The goal is to starve rejection, while at the same time, feed the soil of love, identity and healthy relationships.

It is important to awaken the soldier inside of us, where we can learn to regain areas of our life back from bondage. Here are some beginning practices that are critical for walking in freedom.

1. Honestly assess where a rejection mindset has been in operation. Once the light turns on, your life will never be the same. Coming to a place of personal recognition can be one of the biggest hurdles to climb over. But once you do, you will see in high resolution how much your life and the lives of others have been infested with rejection-based thinking.

You'll need to give God room to show you and reveal how rejection has formed your life and perspective. This can be tricky, because rejection has trained us to live unaware of our true motives.

I recommend that you assume rejection is wanting to influence everything. A number of people I have personally coached, have said, *"I have pretty much realized that rejection tries to get into just about everything, in order to keep me trapped."*

You must begin to recognize that rejection-based thoughts are not even your own thoughts. Rejection is not you, so develop a true lens of who you are so that you can see rejection's lies more clearly. Make rejection the enemy; not yourself, not God and not others.

Begin to notice many of the perspectives you carry that are really rejection-based. Consider what would happen if you made a shift in your thinking to look through a lens that is not based on rejection. Challenge the negative assumptions you normally make of others.

Allow God to take you through a personal inventory without beating yourself up. It can be helpful to write down what you find. As you identify areas that have impacted your life, you can begin praying this prayer out loud:

Father God, I recognize I have had a rejection mindset in the following areas of my life:

_____

_____

2. *Take time to grieve the pain and woundedness.* We have to face the pain that we often ignore, so that we can heal. This involves allowing ourselves to grieve the pain of the past; to process through what we missed in life or what happened to us that damaged us. If we don't, then the pain will follow us in life. So many people self-destruct or have nervous breakdowns because they never deal with the pain they needed to face.

You may even need to engage a *season* of grieving; where you take time to intentionally exchange your pain with God; giving Him your woundedness and receiving His healing touch. I remember one period in my life where it seemed like I was crying or on the verge of crying every day for months. The moment I gave myself permission to let the grieving flow, the more fruitful the healing process became. This season of grieving is necessary, because it takes time for our hearts to process the wounds.

For some, they heal through a brief season, while others take a lot more time. I know most of my wounds took longer than I thought to process out. It often involves times of tears and sorrow, which can be hard for those who live with a stiff upper lip and are uncomfortable with weakness or sadness.

How do we know when it's time to move on from grieving? That is between you and God. It is important to recognize, however, when the tears are not drawing you nearer to healing and closer to God's love, that you may have moved from grief into pity. This is often where you need to stand up, take your peace and move forward. But I also know that we cannot rush the healing process. It needs time, love and personal permission for it to be effective.

3. Take personal responsibility to get free. Only you can take full responsibility for your freedom. Too many are so tuned into rejection's lies, they fail to take responsibility for their lives. We will continue to remain stuck if we place responsibility for our freedom on someone else's shoulders. We cannot continue to point at others as our reason for why we struggle to move forward.

You cannot wait for things around you to change in order to live free. You also cannot wait for others around you to love on you in order to change; otherwise you may end up waiting for the rest of your life. You also cannot wait for people to ask for forgiveness in order for you to move forward.

Taking responsibility for your life is where you start rising up as an overcomer. I suggest you make this declaration out loud:

Father God, I take responsibility for a rejection mindset in my life. I take responsibility for my freedom. I have the ability to make a decision for change and today I choose freedom from rejection!

4. Confront limiting belief systems. A rejection mindset is held in place by a series of limiting beliefs that form your world view under a set of lies. They are designed to keep you trapped, so you will need to confront these limiting beliefs and establish new behavioral patterns.

Rejection is very keen on poisoning your outlook by altering your belief systems. The enemy would love to keep you believing a series of lies that would prevent you from apprehending all that is available to you. Here are some of those lies that drive rejection's work:

- *Bad things always happen to me.*
- *I will never break through.*
- *I always get the short end of the stick.*
- *I can never catch a break.*
- *I can't do this. I am powerless. I can't do this anymore.*
- *I am unlovable.*
- *I don't need anybody.*
- *I have to do life all on my own.*
- *People don't care about me.*
- *I'm not good enough.*

What are the lies in your belief system that need to be handed over to God today?

Father God, I let go of these limiting beliefs in my life:

_____

_____

_____

_____

5. Break agreement with a rejection mindset. Rejection is a spiritual mindset orchestrated by the adversary, so it must be addressed spiritually. In order to do this, we must utilize the gift of repentance, which is how we break off the disempowering agreements we have.

Repentance means moving from one way of thinking and living into another. When we repent, we break agreements that have kept us bound, while moving into new agreements that produce life and freedom. Repentance says, *"I am turning from the ways of rejection. I am putting it behind me. I will no longer listen to rejection's lies. I am now moving towards how God thinks about me."*

I have found it helpful to break agreement with thinking that *"God is far away, He doesn't love me"* or *"He is not near."* Those are some common hooks the enemy uses to keep us locked into rejection.

Repenting from rejection also involves changing our lens in how we see others. Too often we lay the weight of our freedom quest upon someone else finally loving us, accepting us, acknowledging us or giving us what we need. They can become an idol in our hearts that prevents us from true freedom found in God as our source.

Repenting from a rejection mindset breaks the agreements we have that focus on what other people think, performing for others or trying to please their every wish. It positions our hearts to see our relationships with a new set of eyes, where we are not sucked into twisted conversations, division or strife.

Repentance springboards us into a new direction, but it takes time for the new way to take shape. So, don't be discouraged when it doesn't stick overnight. You have to remember that for most people, rejection has been a way of thinking their whole life. Breaking free is not a magical moment that makes everything go away. In fact, I have found that the action which follows my repentance is just as important as the repentant prayer itself.

You will need to revisit your repentance from time to time. That is to be expected. I find that like most areas of our life, repentance from rejection is usually a process more than a one-time experience. It will be important to allow an ongoing work of repentance, because God will show you rejection's work in different areas. We cannot handle dealing with everything at once, so be patient with the process.

Take a moment to use this prayer to repent for the work of rejection. Use the chart in chapter two to reference specific areas of rejection that you want to break agreement with.

Father God, I repent for the work of rejection. I break agreement with its ways in the following areas:

_____

_____

_____

_____

6. Renounce rejection and establish new declarations. Renouncing the work of rejection and its lies is very important in the process of taking back your freedom. Renouncing is a formal declaration. It announces to God, yourself and the enemy your intent to move away from rejection and towards God. What makes renouncing important is that you must say it out loud.

I encourage you to stand to your feet. Go to the park or find a place of solitude, where you can talk freely. You may even have to get in your car to process this out.

Here are some examples of renunciation that further break off the influence of rejection:

- *I renounce serving rejection!*
- *God has not rejected me! He loves me!*

- *I renounce that God is far away. He is very near!*
- *I renounce living as a victim! I renounce self-pity!*
- *I renounce fear! I renounce living as a slave!*
- *I renounce having to do everything perfect!*
- *I renounce performance!*
- *I renounce self-rejection!*
- *I declare that God loves me!*
- *He is for me and not against me!*
- *I refuse to live as a victim! I am an overcomer!*
- *I renounce limitations. I renounce being ignored. I renounce feeling unloved. I am loved. I am accepted. I am dearly loved. I renounce rejection's ways forever!*

In this time of renouncing, you will also need to renounce certain vows that you made, which have reinforced rejection's work in your life:

- *I renounce the vow that I will never cry again.*
- *I renounce the vow that I will never let someone get close to me.*
- *I renounce the lie that I have to do life all on my own.*

Healthy declarations are going to be affirming statements that combat what rejection did.

- *God will never leave me or forsake me.*
- *He loves me and is always here.*
- *I am called to be a son (or daughter) who is loved by my Father.*
- *I am an overcomer!*
- *I am chosen by God!*
- *I am a royal priesthood!*

Write your own renouncements and declarations here:

_____

_____

_____

_____

_____

7. Receive God's forgiveness and love. It is important to position yourself to receive from God, especially His forgiveness and love. Those who have struggled with a rejection mindset often have a hard time receiving, so you will need to be intentional at this stage.

The key is to receive what Jesus Christ paid for. He actually took rejection on the cross, so we do not have to live with the bondage of rejection. You may experience rejection from people, but you do not need to carry a rejection mindset all your life.

He is despised and rejected by men, A Man of sorrows and acquainted with grief. And we hid, as it were, [our] faces from Him; He was despised, and we did not esteem Him. Surely, He has borne our griefs and carried our sorrows; Yet we esteemed Him stricken, Smitten by God, and afflicted. But He [was] wounded for our transgressions, [He was] bruised for our iniquities; The chastisement for our peace [was] upon Him, And by His stripes we are healed. All we like sheep have gone astray; We have turned, everyone, to his own way; And the LORD has laid on Him the iniquity of us all. Isaiah 53:3-6

Jesus experienced rejection. He is aware of what it feels like to be hated or for people to not like Him. He personally experienced what it meant to be unloved, misunderstood, falsely accused and mistreated. He experienced rejection during His ministry in many forms. Most of all, Jesus took that rejection on the cross, so you would not have to live under the deception that a rejection mindset would bring.

It is also important to note that you cannot fully escape being rejected by people. As Jesus was rejected, so will you, especially because He lives in you. But, you don't have to develop a rejection mindset out of it. Too many Christians are seeking to preserve themselves from being rejected by avoiding people, pleasing people or putting up walls. We try to preserve ourselves in the name of safety, but safety in the Kingdom of God is not found in self-protection. True spiritual safety is being secure in the One who loves us and has accepted us completely.

RECEIVING HIS LOVE

When breaking free from rejection, it is important to receive God's love and forgiveness. When we receive the forgiveness of God, we take in His cleansing, but also the power of His love. Experiencing God's forgiveness is one of the ways we can engage God's perfect love for us.

This love is experienced further when I understand who He is as *Abba*; as Dad. The Dad revelation is key here. We've got to be filled with that daily understanding. We can't just keep battling the enemy and not filling those places with the Father's love.

The Bible says, *"We love Him because He first loved us"* (1 John 4:19). So, in processing the love of God, we need to know that *loving God is always a response to receiving His love.*

We don't love Him so that He will love us back. He loved us first! He is the one who started this love exchange. All we need to do is respond to that love by experiencing it and giving it back to Him.

Experiencing the love of God takes an investment of time and slowing ourselves down, to allow our hearts to be positioned in receiving His love. We cannot rush this. In fact, we may have to face some pain in order to cross over into the healing of His love.

I know for me, when I began to thank God for His love, I activated my faith that God's Word is true and that He does love me. I practice this, regardless of what I am feeling at the moment. My faith positions my heart to receive His love. God responds to an act of faith, so begin living in faith that God loves you and He will meet you where you are.

Every believer will process this love uniquely, in different ways and at a difference pace. God knows how you need to receive it, so keep an open heart to the journey of love. As Barry Adams says on FatherHeart.tv,

"Because we are all unique, the way we encounter God's love for us will be as equally unique. The more I get to know God as my Father, the more I realize that He speaks a language that I understand and He knows how to get to the heart of the matter in my life. If you are in a place where you are still waiting for Dad to come home, you are in the best possible place to receive. Just keep waiting and be ready to receive. His love is coming to you!"

When we get a taste of Dad's love, rejection has to go. Father God becomes our validation. Dad is our source.

I suggest you pray this prayer out loud:

Father God, I receive your forgiveness to cleanse me and I take in your love to heal my heart. You are my Father, my Dad and I receive Your love today. Thank you for loving me. In Jesus name, amen.

_____

_____

_____

_____

_____

8. Command the work of rejection to be removed. As you can see, I am a big believer in the power of using your words. They put what we believe into motion. You were designed to have authority over the rejection mindset, not the other way around, so it's important that you command rejection to leave your life in the name of Jesus.

Sometimes it can be good for a brother or sister to pray with you. But most of the time, you have to learn to take your own stand. You can do this by bringing the power of the risen Savior against all forms of rejection that seek to separate you from:

- *The love of God*
- *The identity we have from God in Christ*
- *Our destiny*
- *Our health*
- *Whole and fruitful relationships*
- *A healthy heart full of love to bless others*

Don't be afraid to take your stance and make it known. Be bold and don't back down. You are a loved and accepted child of God!

Here is a sample prayer. I encourage you to make it personal and connect to it from your heart:

In the name of Jesus I command all works of rejection to be broken and removed from my life. I command all the ways of a rejection mindset to leave now. I will not listen to, be bound by or influenced by rejection any longer!

PRAYER

Father God, I recognize where a rejection mindset has had an influence in my thoughts, perceptions and relationships. I take responsibility for freedom today. I repent and break all agreements that I have with rejection. I let go of faulty beliefs systems and perspectives based on rejection that are hindering my growth and transformation.

I renounce listening to the lies of rejection, for allowing it to make me feel separated from God and from other people. I renounce having to perform or strive for love. I let go of having to put up walls or wear masks. I am loved by Father God and receive that today. Rejection is not my friend.

I let go of the slavery that keeps rejection intact. I am not a slave, but a son [daughter] who is loved. I let go of all negative perceptions I carry into relationships or any rejection-based thinking I have of others. Today I declare myself free to love and be loved! I command all works of rejection be broken and removed from my life in Jesus name! Amen

LIVING THE REJECTION-FREE LIFESTYLE

F reedom from a rejection mindset is a process and not just a one-time event. Too often, we over-hype the expectation for sudden breakthrough, while losing appreciation for the daily habits and practices we invest in that produce long term transformation.

Most of what needs change in our lives requires new thinking that we need to sow into on a daily basis. Rejection has become such a part of our thinking and living that we need to allow time to work this out. Be kind to yourself and be kind to others. We need time to learn what it means to be a new creation who is loved and accepted by an amazing Father.

At first, you'll need to be tenacious about cleaning out the rejection mindset. It's like dealing with mold in your house, it can get everywhere and into everything. You have to assume rejection's everywhere, because it is infectious.

I find it takes an all-out assault, because rejection wants to keep you rejected. When you break lose, your options and empowerment go off the charts, but we have to be patient with the healing process.

Don't let yourself become overwhelmed. In fact, whenever you feel yourself starting to emotionally spiral, take a step back and allow patience to enter your heart. We are only able to experience freedom to the level we allow the patience and kindness of God to have a work.

Remember, rejection will place added pressure on you to "get healed" overnight. You will have thoughts that say, *"Why didn't you get over this a long time ago?!"* God is not in a hurry to "get you fixed," so you will need to be patient with your healing process. Any added pressure will only make things harder.

I remember one of my greatest breakthroughs in experiencing transformation was when I gave myself patience to *"take as long as it takes"* in experiencing healing. The moment I took the pressure off to hurry up and get better, I actually accelerated the transformation process. You were not meant to live with that kind of pressure, so don't beat yourself up. Let patience have its work.

BEGIN WALKING FORWARD WITHOUT REJECTION

One of the early questions God spoke to my heart was, *What will life look like without rejection?* This is very different than how most people live. In fact, many people want to be free but don't want to change their lifestyle. It's a myth to think we can experience the transformation available without overhauling how we think and live our lives.

Rejection presents a vision of yourself that is *less than*; where you are unaccepted, unloved and have no potential. Removing rejection not only involves laying down all its lies and casting its work out of our life, it also involves a whole new way of living as dearly loved sons and daughters of God.

CULTIVATING THE NEW MINDSETS

Instead of living out of rejection, we can now live in what rejection was seeking to keep us from. Here are some new mindsets that can take the place of rejection:

- *Instead of a broken heart, we can have a healed, yet sensitive heart.*
- *We can be pressed, but not destroyed.*
- *We can be pierced, but not taken out in bitterness.*
- *Instead of insecurity, practice stepping forward in confidence.*
- *Instead of fear, begin practicing boldness and courage.*
- *Instead of people pleasing, please God and let the chips fall where they may.*
- *Instead of envy and jealousy, practice being happy and rejoice for those you see getting blessed.*
- *Instead of being stubborn, rebellious or pride-filled, humble yourself.*
- *Instead of being driven by an addiction, get filled with the love and acceptance of God.*
- *Instead of assuming the worst in people, begin to assume the best.*
- *Instead of seeing what could go wrong, focus on everything that could go wonderfully!*
- *Instead of being so easily offended, take your peace about others*

and love on them.

- *Instead of defeated and victimized thinking, think from a victorious posture!*
- *Instead of believing you are separated from God, give thanks that He is very near.*

FORGIVING OUR PARENTS

Much of a rejection mindset leads us back to our relationship with mom and dad. I find it important to forgive father and mother for not representing God properly or giving what we needed.

Most of our wounds carry back to our relationship with our parents. We either inherited it from them or our interactions with them spawned a work of rejection.

Either way, we have to move towards a place of forgiving them. If we do not choose to forgive our parents, we will repeat what we did not like about them. Their sin will get permission to repeat in us if we are unwilling to release them. Carrying bitterness or dishonor towards our parents will only keep us in a slave mentality anyway.

Some parents are too toxic or hostile to be around. You may need to love and honor them from a distance, until more peace is available to interact. I have found that many people need seasons of time away from certain family members while they detox the damage. This of course needs to be done with wise council. Don't go into defeat if you need some space to work out your junk that needs processing. Many times, our constant proximity to family can be a door point for keeping us bound, especially since many of the strongholds we battle are the same ones they have.

This is also very important: it can be a mistake to run to our parents for healing. Sometimes when people learn of rejection, they see getting their earthly father or mother's approval as the answer. I have watched people try to get free from rejection by going to their parents for the affirmation they need. Remember, they probably don't have it to give, and at the end of the day, we can only get what we really need from God anyway.

Adjusting expectations of your parents is also very helpful. They only gave what they were given, which for many, wasn't much at all. Broken people who don't heal only repeat brokenness to others. Releasing your parents is a key step in the healing and forgiveness process.

Here is a sample prayer you can use when it comes to forgiveness. I find that forgiving works best if we address the specific area that we are letting go of.

Father God, I choose to forgive my [Dad or Mom] for _____(be as specific as possible). [Dad or Mom] I forgive you for _____(be as specific as possible).

LEARNING TO LOVE YOURSELF

When uprooting rejection from our lives, we can be sure that self-rejection has had its work in teaching us not to accept and love ourselves in peace. We have to remember that God is for us. If He is really for us, then who in the world can be against us?

One of the great ways I can experience God's love is to love myself. The enemy will train us to not be able to accept love from God or others. Yet it is an insult to the cross to not love and accept ourselves as God does.

Self-rejection calls God a liar or says we are too junky to receive love. It's a lying mindset that keeps you from embracing and accepting who you are. We have no reason to reject ourselves, especially when our Creator has not. He loves you and wants you to be at peace with yourself. You are only able to love others in direct proportion to how you love yourself. One of the greatest ways to get free from rejection is to say "yes" to the love that God has for you and love yourself.

THE POWER OF FACING YOUR FEARS

Each of us will have to face the fears that came in as a result of our wounded or unloved areas. To take our identity and relationships back, we cannot let fear run our thoughts any longer. It is one of rejection's best friends, so we need to cast its thoughts far from us.

How do we cast out fear? By accepting God's love and facing our fears, one by one. We cannot run from people any longer. Next time you are in fear, ask God to meet you as you face your fear so that you get to experience what it means to overcome. Most of the time, you will look back and say, *"What was I afraid of all this time?"*

CHANGE YOUR STORY

Everyone with rejection carries a disempowering story that goes along with it. We become bound by that story because it keeps replaying in our thinking. It then gets re-enacted in our decisions and actions.

Make a decision today to change the story over your life. Embrace a new story that involves the provision and love of God in it. Use Paul's exhortation as your guide in what you think could happen in your life:

Finally, brethren, whatever things are true, whatever things are noble, whatever things are just, whatever things are pure, whatever things are lovely, whatever things are of good report, if there is any virtue and if there is anything praiseworthy-- meditate on these things. The things which you learned and received and heard and saw in me, these do, and the God of peace will be with you. Philippians 4:8-9

Take a look at the thought processes you struggle with. Ask yourself, *"What is the story that I am believing here? What has rejection and fear taught me to believe about my life?"* Where can you renounce that old story and pick up God's story for your future?

REHEARSING YOUR NEW IDENTITY

We need constant reminders of who God says we are. We cannot wait for someone else to tell us, we need to practice it. I encourage you to write down what God's Word says about you and make it a part of your daily declarations.

Even if you don't feel it, I still think it's important to say it until you agree wholeheartedly with it. Most people go into their day reacting to whatever happens to them.

Overcomers declare what God says about them. They use their words to empower their day. Every time we fall into temptation or bondage, it is often a result of forgetting who God says that we really are.

The following, based on Ephesians 1 and 2 can be a daily reminder of who you really are:

WHO GOD SAYS I AM

I am blessed with every spiritual blessing in Christ (1:3)

I was chosen before the foundations of the world. (1:4)

I am called to be holy and without blame in love. (1:4)

I am adopted in Christ to Father God. (1:5)

I am accepted in the family of God. (1:6)

I am forgiven. (1:7)

I have a wonderful inheritance. (1:11)

I am sealed with the Holy Spirit of promise. (1:13)

I have a hope and a calling. (1:18)

I am alive. (2:1)

I am seated in heavenly places with Christ. (2:6)

I am God's workmanship. (2:10)

I am created for good works. (2:10)

I have been brought near to God. (2:13)

I am not separated from God. (2:14-18)

I have access today to the Father! (2:18)

In addition, you can craft some custom-made renouncements and declarations that address the specific areas of your life. Here are some examples:

Today I break agreement with all victim based thinking!

I am wonderfully made!

I refuse to live as a victim any longer!

Life will no longer just happen to me. I will happen to life!

I renounce loathing in self-pity!

I renounce feeling sorry for myself!

I will not be a victim to circumstances any longer!

I will not base my happiness on what is happening around me!

I renounce thoughts that God is not with me, He has left me or He has bailed out on me!

God loves me!

I love myself!

I have what it takes to overcome!

Declare these statements at least 3 times a day for 30 days and see what happens. You'll be surprised the power that comes from a believer that connects to what the declaration is saying. In one of my popular teaching recordings, I had everyone in the room yell out *"I am not a victim anymore!"* I have received so much feedback for how that exercise has set people free, empowering them into the identity that God has given them.

LEARNING TO BE YOURSELF

You may not even have a clue as to what the "new you" looks like, but the picture is beginning to form. I want to encourage you to be yourself to the best of your ability wherever you are in your journey. Don't expect yourself to completely arrive, as we are all in process. Take the pressure off to have to "be something" or "be somebody," and give yourself permission to just be yourself.

As Oscar Wilde said, *"Be yourself -everyone else is already taken!"* The best gift you can give to the world is to simply be the YOU God created you to be. Let down your fabrications and masks and let the real YOU shine through!

MOVE FORWARD

As we let go of a rejection mindset, it's time to move forward, based on who we are as sons and daughters of God. More than anything else, God created you to live and breathe, simply as His child. This takes all the pressure off, knowing we are accepted in the family of God by our loving Father. Moving forward as sons removes the yoke of slavery.

Do you know that even when you fail or screw up you're still a son? A son is accepted. His identity never changes. You're a son, you're a daughter! Stop trying to earn it. Stop getting into debate about whether or not you're truly approved. Receive it and begin actualizing your identity today!

RELEASING THE EXPECTATION OF OTHERS

Rejection drives us to be incredibly needy in relationships. It triggers a lot of anger, because people can never be what we want them to be. So today would be a great day to release the expectation of those around you to fill the deep needs of your heart. Many people get stuck in their journey of healing because they put an expectation on others to be something for them.

The fact is people may never be what you need, simply because they cannot fill the God-shaped places in your heart. We need healthy relationships, but there are some places only God can satisfy. If your breakthrough depends on what someone else does for you or how someone else acts towards you, you are in classic codependency. And remember, many of those people are broken too. It's time to do a gut check, release them from these expectations and let God be your source. That way, you can approach people without pressure being placed on them. If they do love you in genuine ways, it becomes icing on the cake.

BE OPEN TO NEW RELATIONSHIPS

In your healing process, there will be a time for you to get back out there again and connect again. It will be time to let people love on you. It doesn't mean you have to let everyone in right away. Take your time, but do your best to get out of isolation and give people a chance. You are better off giving it a try than remaining in the prison of isolation.

It's amazing how God will use various people in our lives to help us understand a tangible revelation of His love. Sometimes those people will come in packages that are not exactly like we are. Be open to this, because God may be trying to show you a facet of His love that you have not understood.

ADJUSTING YOUR STYLE OF RELATING

When rejection works in our lives, it ties us to some unfruitful patterns of relating to people. Maybe it teaches you to shut people down quickly, get angry, isolate, joke too much or become very suspicious. One of the greatest privileges to walking free from rejection is that we get to renew how we relate to others.

This may sound frightening at first, but make it an adventure of starting fresh. Here are some things that can be helpful in learning to relate to others in a new way:

1. Don't jump to conclusions and judge people so quickly. Give them an opportunity to show who they really are. Remember, we are all on this journey of figuring it out.

2. Get rid of suspicion. Many people pride themselves in what they call discernment, but it's really suspicion. It's a protective mechanism, yet it often leads to further paranoia and insanity. Be aware of when you are relying on suspicious thinking and begin to put it away from you.

3. Believe the better intentions of others. Instead of jumping to the conclusion that someone else has a negative motive, why not give them what you would want to be given if you were on their side? Give them the benefit of the doubt. It will make you a more patient person and your relationships will be more fruitful as a result.

BREAKING THE PATTERN

Rejection creates a series of patterns that we often fall into without even noticing. Someone says something, which triggers a rejection response in us and the dominos of dysfunction start falling. I find the only way to break this is to interrupt the pattern we fall into. Sometimes I catch myself and say, *"Wait! No! That's rejection and I am not falling for it! I'm not withdrawing. I am not going into pity. I am not believing that report. I am loved!"*

LOVING ON OTHERS

Don't wait for the day when you are perfectly healed, because you will be highly disappointed. Begin loving others now. Take what you have received and give it out.

It's important to get out of yourself and see the needs of

others. I have found that one of the greatest things God uses in my own healing journey is when I am thinking about and loving on what He cares about, His people.

Love on others, even when it's hard, even though you have been hurt in the past. Many people make it hard to love them, but it does not negate the fact that love works the most powerfully when it is not deserved or welcomed so easily.

It does not mean you need to be a punching bag or chase everyone around with love. I am not telling you to go back into abusive relationships. All I am saying is that when the power of love is tested, you have an opportunity to grow in your spiritual identity like never before.

When someone cannot receive your love, take your peace. Some will and some won't. At the end of the day, whether or not they acknowledge your love is their decision. Sometimes you just have to shake the dust off your feet and move on. Simply be available to love on those God puts in your path. Sometimes the act of love is just accepting where people are at in their journey and releasing them to the process they are in right now.

SOWING INTO YOUR INHERITANCE

The Apostle Paul taught us the value of sowing and reaping, showing us that there is an inheritance waiting for those who know how to sow into blessing.

One area of sowing is into those who have taught us. Paul said, "*Let him who is taught the word share in all good things with him who teaches*" (Galatians 6:6). You can begin to increase your freedom and sow into your inheritance by blessing those who teach you the Word and help you grow in the ways of the Kingdom of God.

It may be a good exercise for you to go back to all those who have invested in your life and find ways to bless them. Send them money. Take them out to eat. Buy them a meal. Write them a letter. Find a way to sow into their lives as a blessing to them and as an investment into your own inheritance that you will leave, ". . . *for whatever a man sows, that he will also reap"* (Galatians 6:7).

I had the chance to send monthly support to a leader who impacted my life during my high school years. He was a great source of instruction and mentoring during my high school days and I am so grateful for it. I know that in walking as a son, my responsibility is to honor those who have invested into my life in many ways.

What does your inheritance look like? Look back and think of all those who have blessed you, showed you love and helped you find who you are. Find ways to bless them. Bless those who have been a blessing to you.

There may have been authority figures in your life that you dishonored or rebelled against. As you walk free of rejection and into what it means to be a son, now would be a good time to seek healthy restoration. You may need to repent to an authority that you were dishonoring towards. Maybe you were in authority and you abused your power towards someone in a harsh way. Why not take this day as an opportunity to make this right and walk in the power of sonship?

CREATE AN ATMOSPHERE OF ACCEPTANCE

In whatever organizations you find yourself apart of

(business, churches or schools), find ways to create atmospheres of acceptance, where people can feel at peace to be themselves. Breathe life into others with your encouraging words. It is in the environment of love where people have the opportunity to change the most. Here are some basic ways we can do this:

- *Show an interest in people's lives and find ways to help them.*
- *Give healthy interactions that make people feel safe.*
- *Smile. It helps a lot.*
- *Make relationships a priority.*
- *Show your love, not just in words, but in action.*

AFFIRMING OTHERS

I find it so valuable to create opportunities to affirm the identity of those around us. I am not just talking about affirming people's performance, although this is important. I am talking about affirming the traits and qualities of God you see in others. There is nothing wrong with "*Good job. Way to go!*" but we need to go deeper and affirm internal qualities of people.

We need to call out those jewels that we see in others, because love has been stirred in our heart towards them. When we stir up love for someone, we can see through their sin issues and see the gold mine of God in their hearts.

LIVING INTERDEPENDENTLY

I mentioned in this book about codependency, where we become tied in an ungodly way to the ups and downs of another person. We make them the source for our self-esteem. I also mentioned the danger of independence, which causes us to withdraw from others and isolate into our own world, preventing us from receiving help or input from healthy people in our lives.

I invite you to begin learning a life of *interdependence*. Let's look at an example of the way this would work between you and me. I come to the relationship already filled up in God, ready to give to you and bless you, with no expectation in return. In addition, you come to me with the same preparation, and we both add value to each other. There are seasons where I am weak and you pick me up. There are seasons where I will do that for you.

This is the body of Christ that Paul talked about in First Corinthians 12, where each body part has a role, empowered by God, and equipped to edify and encourage each other body part. This can only happen when I am personally responsible to get filled up in God and I come to you with a heart to serve you and bless you, not just to receive from you.

THE MINISTRY OF RECONCILIATION

As you become reconciled to the love of God, help others find that same revelation. We need a generation of people who will allow God to heal them, so they can break the work of rejection off of people's lives. We need people in churches, schools, businesses and families who are well equipped to stand in for the many who need healing in these areas of their life. We need people to stand up as spiritual fathers and mothers for this next generation; people who will ask God how He would use them in the days ahead.

Will you be one of those that receive healing from God

and help restore others to Him in Jesus name?

Get out there and live healed and free.

Tell rejection to "take a hike," because God loves you.

I'm cheering you on.

markdejesus.com

Made in the USA
Monee, IL
17 February 2023

28072040R00134